TUNI
MEMOIRS OF A
MIXED MARTIAL ARTS
CHAMPION

Ryan Bow

TUNNEL VISIONS:
MEMOIRS OF A MIXED MARTIAL ARTS CHAMPION

Cover Design by Vanessa No Heart

Published by:
Kaminari Dojo Mixed Martial Arts Academy, L.L.C.
2035 28th St. SE Suite N
Grand Rapids, MI 49508
Website: www.kaminaridojo.com
Email: info@kaminaridojo.com

ISBN: 978-0-9884690-7-5
First Edition
Printed in the United States of America

10 9 8 7 6 5 4 3 2 1

I would like to dedicate this book to my father, Amen Yvon Bow.

Table of Contents

Chapter One

The Destination Begins

Tension was high when I arrived at Korakuen Hall, one of Tokyo's most famous, if compact, fight venues. Over three thousand Tokyoites who clamored for sold-out seating were left to spill into the aisles, corridors and any spot that would afford them even a peek at the battle about to begin below.

His given name was Marcio Barbosa and my first impression was that he was tall and lanky. I expected him to be lethal on the ground as a grappler with a storied guillotine choke, but he would surprise me. Known as "Marcio Cromado" in Japan, I was soon to discover he anticipated this. The strategic Cromado was rumored to be the teacher of the Shooto Lightweight Champion, Alexandre Franca Nogueira. I had seen Cromado choke the former Shooto Champion, Uno Kaoru, into unconsciousness.

Cromado was a luta livre stylist of African ancestry. Luta Livre means wrestling in Portuguese, or more loosely, 'free fighting.' A modern day version of Brazilian judo and wrestling, its flame was lit with the Hatem vs. George Gracie encounter in the 1940s. The sport was later influenced by well-known names such as Fausto, Carlos Brunocilla, Roberto Leitao and the great Nogueira, the current Lightweight Shooto Champion who perfected the guillotine choke.

This was not just another fight. We were the event's main event and while both of us were foreigners, Tokyo had become my second home and that gave me "local" status and crowd backing. My manager, Kobayashi Hidemi, watched from backstage, making sure everything went smoothly. Yamaguchi Mamoru, my corner man, waited patiently with Kobayashi-san, having wrapped my hands and to help me warm up.

There was an eruption of cheering as Cromado and I entered from behind the top row of the audience. He led the way to the ring and I paused, giving his fans a chance to subside. It had become my trademark to dye my hair a new color for every fight and that night's presentation was hidden beneath a hat. I wore the traditional Shooto style compression tights, topped by a burgundy sweatshirt for warmth. As the announcer's voice echoed my name over the loudspeaker, I whipped off the hat to reveal my black and blond creation, complete with the logo of the popular MMA clothing, "Bad Boy" etched across the back. "Move Bitch" by Ludacris boomed over the crowd's cheers and I remember absorbing their excitement and tension. Cromado wouldn't look me in the eye; perhaps he sensed I was ready for battle. Perhaps that's what molded his strategy. I chose to believe his behavior signaled weakness.

The fight finally began and it soon became apparent that Cromado had decided to begin his assault with an uncharacteristic kickboxing approach. However, while posturing early on, his finger poked me in the eye, blurring my vision. My strategy of aggressive punches and kicks was left behind as I buckled in to grind out the win.

The spectre of Cromado's unconscious choking of the former champion flitting through my memory, our match was fought clinched against the ropes. I drove indecision from my world of focus and saw my opportunity to finally get the takedown and top position. Launching a vicious ground and pound from inside his guard position, the hard-fought match ended in a win that earned me the Shooto Welterweight Number 1 ranking. The crowd exploded in prideful, triumphant cheers as the dismantled Cromodo left the hall. The "local" candidate had taken the March night and won hearts in the process.

I had come so far to reach this destination, only to realize that my journey had just begun. I had come a long way from Grand Rapids…

* * * * *

It was the memorably frigid February of 1979 in Grand Rapids, Michigan. Nearby, Lake Michigan had frozen over almost completely for the first time on record. 80 miles wide, you could walk across it to Milwaukee over the crystallized shipwrecks languishing in its murky, ice-capped depths.

It was the second night of the month when an alarmed mother frantically rushed to the nearest hospital. Her son, who wasn't due to be born for another 43 days, was fighting to make an early entrance. She did not know then that this signaled the first of his many battles against daunting odds. Perhaps it was his communication of fear and anticipation that drove her to the hospital that night; a premature, but prescient fight that even his father recognized.

The next day Amen and Diane Bow's caution was rewarded as a premature, but healthy, Ryan Christopher Bow was put into their arms. Despite the early entry, it appeared I was completely healthy. Our young family's life would never be the same.

Chapter Two

Strong Roots

Diane Belinda Hall loved to play the piano. The eldest of five children, she was born in Ypsilanti, Michigan to parents who taught them the value of self-discipline, a respect for authority and a love of God. Diane's parents insisted each of their children study a foreign language for at least two years. Later, Diane would put this to good use, as she became a teacher of the fluid and romantic French language.

Diane, my mother, grew up privileged, in a home full of loving support partnered with strict discipline. The library, scouting and church were encouraged; dating and parties were not. When eventually she was allowed to date, curfews on Saturday night were strictly enforced, as was attendance at Sunday morning services the next day.

College was not optional. My grandmother had graduated from Alcorn College in Mississippi. After their marriage, my grandfather insisted she give up her career and stay at home with their children. My grandmother resented this and as their family home was situated along an otherwise deserted country road, her options were limited. Thus, my mother and her siblings were college-bound, like it or not.

They say that opposites attract and perhaps that was true when it came to my parents. They had met at Ypsilanti High School near the end of their tenth grade years where my father was also an excellent high school wrestler. Good enough, in fact, to earn an invitation to the Olympic camp. Finances, along with a few other issues, cruelly rendered him unable to pursue the dream of training alongside our country's best and brightest wrestlers. It was a huge disappointment, but my father was never one to dwell on the past or let roadblocks slow him down. If something didn't go his way he simply shrugged it off and got on with life.

As fate would have it on one cold wintery afternoon in November, Dad happened to be brushing up on his history in the study hall and happened to sit next my mother's good friend, Sandra. He looked past Sandra at my mother and their eyes met in an awkward way. He was never known as a "talker" but nor was he timid. The two of them got talking and, as the story goes, Sandra bet my dad fifty-cents that my father wouldn't have the nerve to call my mother for a date. Of course, Sandra would lose that bet. Dad wasn't very forward when it came to pretty girls, but he eventually worked up the nerve to ask Mom out. In fact, during summer break that year, my father called my mother almost every day. Before long he was hooked on her. The two of them dated through most of high school as well as their years at Michigan State University.

My father's family was considerably larger; he was the youngest of 15 children. Appropriately so, his mother named him "Amen" even before knowing whether he would be a boy or girl, and prayed that this would be their last child. My father's family attended the Mt. Olive Church of God in Christ in the Pentecostal faith. His upbringing was also strict, but in the sense that there were mandatory dress codes, makeup was not permitted, girls must wear dresses and could not cut their hair once they had been "saved." This branch of my family was considerably less affluent and made their home in the city. Despite the difference in their backgrounds, my parents were married on August 2, 1975; a candlelit wedding that was considered an event, clad in white and the bride's favorite pink.

Their young married life was joyful when I joined it. This was about to change dramatically, especially for my mother.

My grandmother, whom I called Nana, developed breast cancer. She required two mastectomies within four months.

Despite the fact that my mother was teaching and caring for me as a young child, she also became the primary caregiver for her mother. Each weekend she travelled to Ypsilanti to see to Nana's needs, leaving at 5 a.m. on Monday mornings to be in her classroom by 8:15. After nine years, my grandmother lost her battle and passed on just before Christmas in 1983. My mother's sister, Aunt Donna, had not yet even graduated high school at the time.

My grandfather was a World War II veteran and I was always proud of that. He grew up in the South during very hard times. As we all know, hard times can strengthen what we're really made of. He only had an 8th-grade education, but made a good living in spite of that. He owned and ran his own business, which consisted of two successful barbershops; one in Ann Arbor and one in Ypsilanti. Like my grandfather, I was always more interested in setting the pace rather than trying to keep up with everybody else. He was a great inspiration in my life.

Exhausted and grieving for the parent who had been strict in the most loving manner, my mother consequently fell into a deep depression. She was trying to help her younger sister make college plans, against their father's wishes. The depression was relentless and she desperately wanted to see her mother again and be free of the pain. On Thanksgiving of 1984, my mother penned a suicide note as she finished cooking the family dinner. My father became instantly alarmed and phoned her psychologist. This launched what was to be the first of several hospitalizations for depression; the longest of seven month's duration.

Despite our secure and loving family life, my mother's condition worsened to the extent that it seemed she was out of control of her actions at times and needed to be hospitalized. I can recall on one occasion her carving the words "HATE" and "DEATH" into her skin with a kitchen knife and my father frantically consoling her to save the situation. Somewhat inevitably, incidents like this meant she had to quit working and be hospitalized.

While in the hospital, mom sometimes went through shock therapy and had to be restrained in a straightjacket—a truly horrible situation for all of us.

Despite all this turmoil, my father held the family together. Dad continued to work hard and made sure he and I went to visit my mother in the hospital as often as possible.

She would finally be released and, over time, would learn to control her occasional mood swings. My mother was eventually diagnosed as bi-polar with manic depression and even to this day must take a myriad of medications to function. These medications alter brain chemicals and their side effects alone are unstable and overwhelming.

I wasn't aware of it then, but I learned that growing up around bi-polar disorder can cause disconnection in young children; an unwillingness to understand people's problems. It could also have been one of the reasons I always felt the need to "get away" someday.

I was young. Along with that came an unwillingness to even try and understand her disease. Instead I just wanted to get away. But we held it all together and life went on.

Both my mother and father were amazing people who were destined for a great life. They quite simply never gave up, believing that no matter what life dished out in the way of obstacles, love and hard work would forever overcome such hurdles. My early years growing up were fantastic to say the least! Not only was my family middle class, but also I was an only child. My parents had a tendency to spoil me rotten. I didn't realize they were spoiling me at the time, but whatever they were doing, my life couldn't have been more perfect. Punishments were rare; my mother remembers me as a well-behaved child with good values who needed very little correction.

Perhaps growing up in such an environment was one of the reasons I was seldom exposed to hardship outside my own immediate family. I grew up at a time when families just dealt with their problems and left others to theirs. As far as I was concerned, life was good for me, so life must have been good for everyone.

My father was the football and wrestling coach at Ottawa Hills High School where he also taught English. He was loved and well respected by all his students. My mother, meanwhile, taught French at Union High School. Even though my mother had never been a sports fan, the two of them were very involved in school activities as well as in everything else in my life.

Dad wanted to start me out wrestling at an early age, but once I saw the movie, *The Last Dragon*, I knew what kind of wrestling I wanted to do; and it wasn't rolling around on some mat with a guy in tights. It was called… *kung fu*! Even at six-years-old, I knew exactly what I wanted to be when I grew up and when I made my mind up to do something, I usually did it. Watching that movie inspired me in ways I can't even explain. The plot consisted of a young boy who, against all odds, was able to triumph and win the day. Not only did he win the day, but also he won it with style and raw emotion.

I recall that usually when my father was coaching at wrestling matches, my mother would stay home and take care of me. This was very hard on Mom, but she always took it in her stride and somehow got everything done, despite her disability.

Eventually, though, the schedule became too much, and the strain of it was having an effect on our family. Consequently, my father stopped coaching wrestling to spend more time at home. Both my parents made it a point to always be in my life and, more than that, to be a big part of my life. I think their love and commitment played a part in shaping the man I have become, giving me the priceless strong foundation upon which to build my success in the most fearsome of professions.

I was always more of a leader growing up and never much of a follower. I attribute this to how my parents brought me up; but also that I most likely inherited one of the strong personality traits that helped my grandfather to succeed.

My father was loving and supportive of my mother and I. My mother is still active and her smiling face is a testament to strength and endurance.

Chapter Three

Falling in Love

When you ask a ten-year-old boy what he wants to be when he grows up, you might expect that he wants to follow his father's footsteps. He might choose to be a policeman, a fireman or even president. Not many want to be Bruce Leroy. I did.

Now a cult classic, *The Last Dragon* was a 1985 martial arts production starring Taimak as Bruce Leroy. This Barry Gordy production was highly relatable as Gordy was a fellow Michigander. The character, Bruce Leroy's, quest in life was to achieve the highest level of martial arts accomplishment. This was known as "The Final Level" and when achieved, the fighter's hands would glow. Only when you become the greatest fighter alive would your entire body glow. I wanted to be Bruce Leroy and saw myself in the role as naturally as if I were watching my own future unfold.

That's not to say my father's athletic inclinations didn't influence me; they certainly did. But when my friend, Dave, invited me to do some sparring in his front yard, I fell in love…with martial arts.

As a youngster I was interested in all the things other little boys are interested in; running, jumping, just having an all-round good time. Dave had been studying taekwondo for some time and the opportunity to try out new moves on me was irresistible. I didn't mind since I was always interested in the martial arts, anyway. Better still, it was like being in the movie *The Last Dragon*. I knew I wouldn't be much of a sparring partner for Dave yet, but I still wanted to see what I could do; after all I'd seen Taimak Guarriello (Bruce Leroy) kick butt more than a hundred times in the movie, so I was prepared. After all, with all the grandeur of a major martial arts musical film as your future, who was I to deny my self-endowed talent?

Summers in Michigan are often warm but seldom terribly humid. Lake Michigan tempers the incoming weather from the west and adds its own breezes. Dave's front yard was sheltered beneath massive oak trees and it was here that we punched and kicked for hours. Even though most of my strikes never found their mark, my interest was once again piqued. I was fascinated by the acquired, albeit amateur, skills Dave was demonstrating and the images of *The Last Dragon* filled my imagination. By the time he was through kicking my butt all over the yard, I was hooked for good. It was also there on that shade-mottled front lawn that I realized, even with my limited knowledge and skill, I was still able to compete with Dave and make a few good moves myself. Sure he landed everything, and I landed next-to-nothing, but I was still good. I could feel it inside and it triggered something almost primeval in me. I just lacked any actual technique when it came to fighting but that could and would be fixed.

Even from a young age, I was a very competitive person. I hated losing. My father and I shared this quality, and he was always at my side. Whether I was playing football, baseball or competing in martial arts tournaments, he was always the first to arrive, and the last to leave. True to his coaching skills, when I couldn't do something, he spent the extra time teaching me how; one-on-one. His passion showed when I competed; you could hear him cheering me on above any other voice.

~

I think being competitive means one is born with a hatred for defeat.

~

I think being competitive means one is born with a hatred for defeat. It shows in the ring, or in the cage when you fight. Many times, a person will give up mentally. When I was young, my father's patience helped me learn and be competitive. As the last of fifteen children, competition was something my father understood. As I would learn later on when I was living alone in Japan, the sheer *need* to eat and do well was motivation enough.

I have a tendency to become obsessed with improving myself in anything I failed at in the past. Even to this day, I am the same way. I spent all my free time researching the possibilities and learning from the best, and closest teacher.

By the time I was ready to enter my sophomore year at Ottawa Hills High School in Grand Rapids, my parents allowed me to join a martial arts school called *Chan's Kung Fu School*, where I began learning wing chun and judo. I spent the majority of time at the Kung Fu School. My friends became the people I trained with. Duncan was ten years older; a big brother of sorts. He was definitely someone I looked up to. We developed a close friendship and I later went to Hong Kong with him. He was my *senpai*, which is Japanese for *my senior*.

The Japanese society is based on time-honored tradition. Most Americans cannot relate to this as our relatively modern government is just over 200 years old and we've attracted new citizens from all over the world. Where the first humans are believed to have travelled to the mainland U.S. about 15,000 years ago, the same migration to the Japanese islands happened almost three times that long ago. Wherein the U.S. has always offered lands for exploration and expansion, the Japanese Islands have always been far more densely populated and the lands are quite limited.

These factors have led to a societal commitment for preservation and appreciation. Thus, when an elder or more accomplished man is addressed, it is with great respect and reverence; hence the title *senpai* is used to indicate this deference.

There is a competitive bias between the countries in Asia. Each has a sense of national pride; each is deeply steeped in its own culture and history, which has, at times, made them fiercely competitive with one another. This contributed, certainly, to the development of martial arts in that these societies are quite ancient and have valued self-defense first as superior wit and individual skill, and then followed by weaponry. By contrast the Western cultures have developed defenses based on machinery and technological advancement. These differences reflect the historical perspective that Western philosophies have included exploration, colonization and the broadly held belief that the rest of the world is needful of American principles. Years later I would come to strongly dislike this view of the world. The countries of the Orient look more toward conservation and individual improvement. Japan has occupied parts of Korea and China in the past, a fact that is resented by many in these countries. This is true of Japan, as well as China. Each is fiercely proud and nationalistic, yet they do share the values of respect. For example, the concept of *senpai* exists in both nations, although in parts of China it is termed *si hing*, or "elder kung fu brother." Kung fu is Chinese in origin.

Thus, *Chan's Kung Fu School* was an introduction to not only the techniques of the sport, but the exposure to a time-honored culture. It was here that I could finally learn how to fight like the guys on television and in the movies. This was the first step toward realizing one of my greatest dreams. Thus it was that kung fu became the next rung on the ladder I would climb to success.

Another well-known martial arts figure, Bruce Lee, although born in San Francisco's Chinatown, returned with his parents to Hong Kong when he was just three-months-old. This famed martial artist, teacher and film star of five feature-length films was initially trained in wing chun under Yip Man. This tutorship ended when Yip Man's other students refused to train beside Lee; as tradition dictated that their arts not be taught to anyone of non-Asian ancestry. Lee's mixed blood (his mother was Catholic and of a mixed German and Chinese ancestry) made him an outsider. Lee held dual Chinese and American citizenship and at the age of 18, returned to the U.S. to take the 1957 High School Boxing Championship. He went on to found jeet kune do, his personal martial arts philosophy.

It was then that to my delight, I discovered an authentic martial arts teacher from Hong Kong teaching right there on Division Street in town. This was more than I'd dreamed was possible. In my young impressionable mind, just being from Hong Kong gave him tremendous credibility. He was Sifu Sam Hing Fai Chan and the thought of training with such a teacher sent chills down my young spine. Parts of Division Street are in an area where gang violence occasionally occurs. The kung fu school was about a mile from the more dangerous part, but not an upscale area, by any means.

Suddenly everything I wanted to be was within the range of my young, trembling fingertips. The thought of learning martial arts filled me with anticipation rivaled only by Christmas. This was also the year that I discovered mixed martial arts (MMA) and knew I'd discovered the stuff of fantasy.

As a full contact sport, mixed martial arts allow both grappling and striking. Its roots date to the original Olympics and were in the sport of pankration. These mixed style contests could be found in the early 1900s in Japan, Europe and along the Pacific Rim. By the 1990s, the combat sport of vale tudo from Brazil entered the U.S. scene and the Ultimate Fighting Championship (UFC) was born.

I was only fifteen when my father and I ordered pay-per-view to watch the UFC clash where Royce Gracie would win the tournament, proving for the second time that Brazilian jiu-jitsu was the most effective art in the sport. It was right after watching that fight that I began my judo lessons. Christmas had, indeed, arrived early.

Like anyone connected to the sport at the time, I was very eager to learn more about this martial art and particularly zealous in incorporating it into the kung fu and judo skills I was learning. My friend, Nick, a fellow wing chun student, would practice the moves we saw on television with me for hours on end. We did most of the practicing on the floor in his living room, but that didn't matter to me.

At that time, there were no Brazilian jiu-jitsu schools in Grand Rapids. Even many professional fighters had to either rely on videotapes to learn the techniques, or travel to one of the few places with a reputable instructor. The Midwest had been trying to catch up in this regard from the beginning. In those days, most of the Brazilians who came to America to teach chose to open schools in California.

Committed to the sport, I had the burning desire to practice and perfect the techniques at any opportunity I got. I was going to be better than Dave, Nick, Bruce Leroy; perhaps some day even better than the great Bruce Lee himself. I was determined that nothing would slow me down.

That was, however, not completely within my control. Life takes its own turns, as I was about to find out.

Chapter Four

Reality Hits

It was 1995. Something was deadly wrong with my brain.

I was working at a local pet store, *Chow Hound*, at the time. On my way home one evening, my vision must have become blurred or distorted for a few moments because I somehow managed to sideswipe another car without even seeing it. It was as though it had simply dropped down from the sky. Fear paralyzed me as I heard the rending of metal on metal and the squeal of brakes on the pavement. I'm not sure what made me panic the most; the terror that I was about to become human wreckage or the stunned, dropped-off-the-cliff realization that there was a car where I had seen nothing but air.

The feeling is difficult to describe. People have, what I often describe as, some sort of sixth-sense, or feeling. Many times, even though you cannot see something, you can feel its presence. I can probably explain this best as that awareness you have when someone walks silently up behind you yet you know they're there by the energy field they emit. I do not have this "feeling" or sensory perception on my left side. In strict medical terms it could be considered insensibility— not due to any emotional or intellectual deficiency—simply a result of the brain's insufficient sensory balance on the my left side. It can be very frustrating, for example, when I'm driving and cars turn into my lane ahead of me by coming in from my left. It is so unexpected that it makes me catch my breath.

After that accident, I did the only thing that could make it worse. I panicked and made a quick, regrettable decision. I ended up speeding away from the scene out of fear and confusion. I couldn't think of consequences; only that

I needed to find a safe place to figure out what had just happened. The other driver, however, was far less confused. He followed me home and there was suddenly nowhere to hide.

This was completely out of character for me, so I was devastated when I realized what I had done. *What was happening and how did I hit what seemed to be an invisible car?*

Crying hysterically, I screamed in frustration that I had never seen the car; that I had no idea where it came from and that I wasn't to be blamed. The other driver looked doubtful and I couldn't really blame him. Young males are notoriously careless and headstrong drivers. I could see my future with a huge roadblock; higher insurance, possibly lose my license since I left the scene of an accident and that would definitely result in my losing my job. Life, as I knew it, was on the line. I pleaded with my parents and stressed my innocence.

"I swear," I yelled, "I never saw the car!"

Their response was incredulous. *What happened to the person in the other car? Were you ticketed for leaving the scene? Was the other driver angry? What was the weather like?* I could see the questions in their eyes and while they wanted to defend me in front of the other driver, they had to be dutifully outraged that I'd run away from my responsibility. My mother wore a suspicious frown and my father's hands nervously fiddled with change in his pocket. This wasn't just a question of my having made a bad decision; this involved their ability to trust my word.

With some heated discussion, it turned out that the other driver lacked car insurance and that added to his anger. However, it happened that one of the other passengers was a former student of my father's and they came to an amicable settlement without involving the police. My parents paid for the damage to both vehicles. That didn't end the discussion, however.

The weather that evening had been clear; no rain and it had still been light when it occurred. There was no explanation for my lack of vigilance and as I kept claiming innocence, I could see the concern in my parents' face. They knew me and wanted to believe I wasn't a liar; at least not on matters such as this. In fact, I was so adamant about it that my parents thought it would be a good idea to have my eyesight checked. So that's exactly what we did, in the way that parents look for some sort of delay in handing out sentence, hoping for that remote chance of exoneration.

It came just that way, and from the doctor's mouth. It wasn't, however, quite that simple. We were informed that I was peripherally blind. In fact, I had been so since birth. There was zero peripheral vision on the left side of either eye, which was why I never saw the car. *Really* never saw it! In more well known terms, this meant I suffered from tunnel vision. It's far more common in older people with glaucoma or brain damage after a stroke. I was about to learn what had happened to me.

This unusual condition prompted my parents to seek advice from a neurologist. In our family, this meant a heavyweight sort of doctor. There was very little a neurologist could say that would be helped with an aspirin.

His office rested in one of the adjunct office buildings near the hospital downtown. It smelled of sterile alcohol and cleaning chemicals, but represented something far more terrifying. I remember looking at the walls of the hallway and wondering if these would be the landscapes for my final days.

The doctor lacked bedside manner and I could sense the fear in my mother, even though she was doing her best to appear calm for me. At that point, it was theorized that since both my eyes evidenced the same handicap, the problem was most likely somewhere in the brain. That was the last thing anyone wanted to hear. Brain issues were always serious.

This was before laser or computer-guided microsurgery. My only consolation was that at least a lot of awkward moments in my life now began to make perfect sense. Suddenly I understood why I had bumped into things for no apparent reason. As an example, while walking down a street or in stores, I often bump into people passing by in the opposite direction. This happens most often in crowds.

While it certainly was mixed news to hear about my health issues, it explained so much. There is redemption in knowing that not everything is your fault. In one sense, it gives you the motivation to overcome what you now understand. But at the age of 16, with a future of martial arts firmly set in my mind, this was a difficulty I had never anticipated. It brought with it an essential instinct of fear. I was afraid of how it could affect my martial arts training.

Then there was an MRI to consider. This had been ordered to give the neurologist a roadmap to my brain. I had no clue how claustrophobic it would be lying inside a circular machine resembling something out of an old sci-fi movie flick. The thing even made groaning and buzzing sounds as it circled around me like some orbiting space station. It was tight and claustrophobic. I felt lost. The noise, the isolation and knowing I couldn't back out. I had to stay until the end. I was alone with my thoughts. *Why is this taking so long? I feel like I'm about to have a panic attack.* After about 45 agonizing minutes, the ordeal ended. I stared at the faces of the attendants, trying to tell if they had seen something dreadful and were saving the bad news for the doctor to tell. Did their eyes carry pity when they looked at me, or worse yet, were they avoiding my eyes entirely? It seemed their responses were forced and too lighthearted. W*hat did they know and weren't allowed to say*? I felt like the doomed man in a Saturday night movie. I began to mentally draft my will and could picture all my friends from the gym standing around my hospital bed sniffing while they began to click off the life support machines. I wanted so badly to hit or kick something. Instead, we went home and waited for what seemed like a lifetime.

Instead, I spent that "lifetime" of waiting in training. There was a feeling of being powerless, so I did the one thing that I *could* control – and that was to train kung fu. If there was bad news coming, it would be here soon enough.

My good friend, Duncan, and I would always go at each other pretty hard whenever we sparred together. During that waiting period, Duncan caught the result of my worry and frustration. It was okay, though; he seemed to understand something was terribly amiss in my life.

I remember a few days after my testing, just before working out together. I happened to mention what was going on with my head. I vividly recall the look of shock and confusion that flashed across his face like a lightning bolt. Thinking back, I shouldn't have been surprised at all by his reaction, but suddenly Duncan tried his hardest *not* to hit me when we sparred. I knew exactly where he was coming from, but I loved to spar and knowing that my opponent was never going to strike back… well, it just wasn't the same.

~

It seemed I had a cyst—and one that would require brain surgery.

~

Once the results were in, they were like a bomb dropped from the sky.

It seemed I had a cyst—and one that would require brain surgery. The cause of the accident and my protests of not having seen the car had, indeed, been in my head; but not in the sense most people mean. The doctors would place a shunt in my brain to drain the cyst. It would take place in months, if not weeks. Furthermore, the results would not be certain.

The surgery would be tricky and the results embedded with side effects. The odds were not in my favor. I yearned to be guilty of poor driving again; at least for that I could take my punishment and move on. But not now, not knowing what we now faced. What I faced. I longed to again be innocent. Somehow the period of waiting had felt better.

There are five different kinds of brain cysts and they are all complicated. Cysts grow and can wrap themselves around the brain itself, cutting off the blood supply. This was before the days of the Internet and there was little information out there to give us something to cling to. After all, even those who survived weren't always able to still talk about their experience.

This wasn't supposed to happen to me. These things happened to other people; to those dirty guys who lie against the curb with cheap wine bottles stuffed into greasy paper bags. This happened to disheveled old people who soiled their pants and drooled in oblivion. This happened to children living next to toxic waste dumps; their eyes sunken and blackened beneath balding heads due to rounds of chemotherapy that might just give them ten more months to live. This didn't happen to people like me; this didn't happen in my family.

But, it had. Terrified, and after some deliberation, both my parents felt it best to hold off with the operation for as long as possible. They also wanted to get a second opinion. They brought in a well-known neurosurgeon and her opinion did little to set their minds to rest. She explained that if the cyst were filled with blood, there was a potential for it to rupture and that could kill me. If, however, the cyst were filled with spinal fluid, the outlook was somewhat brighter. The irony was lost on us.

As it turned out, the latter was true; my dark cloud had been fitted with a temporary silver lining. The neurosurgeon added that had we known about this when I was born, I would not have lived a normal life. I would not have been able to play sports because most kids who have a cyst similar to mine have some form of cerebral palsy.

Even though the experience was terrifying for my entire family, in hindsight my parents were looking out for me and made the best decisions possible. There is nothing to compare to the fear a parent feels when their child's life is in danger. It is the stuff of hellish nightmares. There were so many questions, very few answers and absolutely no guarantees. It turns out that most likely I'd had a stroke when I was in the womb and that it was nothing short of a miracle that I wasn't left handicapped in some way. A small portion of my brain had actually died and my body had filled that empty area with a cyst filled with spinal fluid. That was good news, too, but somehow it carried little weight in relieving my mind. What would I do? I was a martial artist!

The specialist, who was sympathetic, pointed out that my brain would be more vulnerable and I would be more susceptible to a knockout. She understood my disappointment and went on to say, "Go after your dream."

When I should have been counting my blessings, all I could think of was what this meant to my martial arts. I was now handicapped and even if I was able to fight again; I would be at a tremendous disadvantage. My diagnosis meant that all contact sports could be a thing of the past.

Not only was I affected because I couldn't see things clearly from my left side, but every punch, every kick and every blow I sustained would affect my equilibrium in a greater way than it would affect my healthy opponent. The possibilities of what could happen to me by getting punched, thrown and kicked in the head numerous times were also too monstrous to contemplate.

The grim prognosis was impossible to ignore, but that is exactly what I chose to do. Although engagement in MMA could leave me with permanent brain damage due to a ruptured cyst, I wasn't willing to give up on my dream. There was a high risk that it could mean my being crippled and unable to fend for myself.

My choice was to take the giant ball fate had thrown me and throw it back. The path I was about to choose would determine my life. Despite the defect in my brain, I had the heart of a warrior; just like my father. I wasn't going to let a few roadblocks hold me back from where I wanted to go. I would pursue my American dream no matter how terrifying the potential cost.

Was I scared? You know it. However, I firmly remember lying in bed one night thinking that dying in the ring would be better than not pursuing my dreams. I wanted it very badly, even at the risk of sacrificing my life.

The uncertainty of being unable to pursue my dreams had a cold grip on my heart. Defiant, I remember on one occasion, hitting myself in the head with a closed fist to prove to myself that I could withstand the bodily harm that comes from competing. Obviously, this was not a healthy reaction. But, at the time, I could not imagine a life without martial arts in it. I didn't know how to deal with the frustration of it all. Counseling may have helped, but my situation was fairly unique.

In hindsight, my thought process was very naïve, but that's how I felt at the time.

Chapter Five

Black Belts vs. Brain Damage

While my condition was of great concern and the risks were considerable, I was determined not to let it affect my life. My chief goal was to become a great martial artist and fighter. To not follow my dream would mean an even greater devastation. In my young mind it could only be compared to Bruce Leroy losing in the finale of *The Last Dragon*.

My parents were understandably concerned with my decision to pursue a career that could potentially end my life, but were always very supportive of whatever decision I made. It must have been very difficult for them, but what an amazing ability they had to allow me my own space. To allow your only child to place their dream above the tremendous risk at hand was truly an act of selfless bravery. That did not compare, though, with the selflessness they were about to demonstrate.

I spent hours a day at my kung fu school learning and studying every movement of both wing chun and judo. By this time, my grades had gotten worse in school because I'd stopped applying myself. I'd made up my mind. I wanted to pursue a career in the martial arts and training was more important to me than homework. Instead, I trained.

Perhaps it was the act of throwing caution to the wind with regard to my brain cyst that emboldened me to put my education at such a low priority.

~

Having a broad education was great for the average individual…but I wasn't interested in being average.

~

My predicament helped to form a foundation of what I believe even to this day. Traditional education is good for most but, for me, it couldn't help me achieve my dreams. As a youth, I felt it even hindered me. I would rather spend the time wasted in school in training instead. Having a broad education was great for the average individual. I wasn't interested in being average, however, and there was no college degree in martial arts.

I became more determined now than ever. I could no longer afford to simply be good; I had to be great. There was no settling. Although my handicap would always fight at my side, I needed to compensate by being significantly better than my opponent in every conceivable way.

Having just discovered that I had tunnel vision, I was initially a bit spooked by the idea of being impaired. I didn't allow the cyst to worry me, but I knew that I had a visual weakness that could be exploited by an opponent. What would I not see coming? Which moments when he let his guard down would be overlooked?

I learned to punch better and to kick harder. I learned to throw and grapple to the extent that I eventually earned my red sash in wing chun and my green belt in judo. I trained harder and paid more attention to detail because I knew I was at a disadvantage and needed to even things up.

I had to become smarter and faster than my opponents. The martial arts require as much thought as they do physical skill. Modern day psychology is no longer discounting the effects of martial arts training as they once did. They've conducted studies with control groups that indicate that using the combination of guided imagery with martial arts self-defense techniques can significantly lower anxiety and depression. Curiously, however, these effects are not realized until a martial artist has studied for some time. In fact, students are found to have a heightened sense of anxiety during their initial stages of training.

Perhaps it was this heightened anxiety that propelled me into what many would consider, a reckless decision. In my young mind, however, the only way I could level the field was to be a superior fighter in every way. That was my driving force and my goal.

Superiority required speed and strength. My kicks needed to hit their mark the first time. When I grappled, the act of wrestling with an opponent, I needed to be in total control and never let my adversary get the upper hand and reverse me. This was how I planned to fight; this was how I planned to win and this was how I planned on keeping my cyst under control. I believe at that stage I envisioned my cyst and my opponent as equal forces. Each had to be rendered harmless.

In 1996, about two years after starting kung fu and judo, I discovered that my *sifu*, my martial arts instructor, was going to Hong Kong with a few other students. When I found out about the trip, of course I wanted to go along. I asked my parents and to my surprise they didn't put up much opposition. To allow their son to physically distance himself when they knew how fragile his life could be was truly a remarkably courageous and loving act.

So after discussing this with my *sifu*, it was all set. As a result, shortly after my 17th birthday, I was off to Hong Kong to encounter a culture much different from anything I had ever experienced or imagined in my life. It would leave me with a lasting impression even today.

* * * * *

I signed out of school and we were about to be off to Hong Kong for two weeks. My parents paid for the trip and looking back on it, I see that I was privileged. In one sense, this would make it harder for me to be on my own when I travelled later in life. We flew from Grand Rapids to Chicago, Chicago to Korea, and then from Korea to Hong Kong. There were no overnight layovers.

It wasn't my first time flying. My parents, unlike those of most of my friends, had a higher vision for me and that included taking trips to see the world while I was young. I had travelled Europe including London, Paris, Germany and France, and more.

It had been probably eight years since our last trip and this was my first trip to Asia. The trip to Hong Kong was short, but meaningful. There was my *sifu*, Brad and Duncan, who unlike me were all adults. I remember arriving at the airport filled with excitement and anticipation.

It was February in Hong Kong, but it felt more like July in the tropics. It was hot and oppressively humid. As a young kid from Michigan, I wasn't accustomed to that kind of climate. That alone consumed my attention on the first day there. You could even smell the humidity, swelling in swirls of smoke and the odor of too many human beings in a small space.

Hong Kong is located in eastern Asia between China and the South China Sea. It's roughly six times the size of Washington, D.C. and has what is defined as a subtropical monsoon climate. Lowlands in the north meet hilly and sometimes mountainous slopes. Its deep-water harbor has helped gain its reputation as a world-class port. It is a city of excess, composed of more than 200 islands dampened with air and water pollution.

Sifu and Duncan arrived a day earlier than we did. They met Brad and I at the airport in Hong Kong late in the evening. It was crowded in this fast-paced, predominantly Asian city. I was too uncomfortable to even be excited; taking everything in and feeling overwhelmed. There were more people scurrying around than I'd ever seen in my life.

As it was his hometown, *Sifu* had made all the arrangements. We shared a single sleeping room in a hostel and tried to fall into an exhausted sleep despite the traffic and construction noise. Hong Kong is often referred to as a concrete jungle. Its building boom has added dimensional growth within the existing borders; buildings swallow the landscape.

I had been brought up to be polite. Thus, I stopped to let a few women go ahead of me, but was instantly scolded and told in no uncertain terms that I did not need to let women go ahead of me.

In East Asian countries, at least in China and Japan as I would discover later, it is not the custom to hold doors open for women or to let them enter first. I'm certain there are times when one might do it anyway, but in a busy place where everyone is always in a big hurry to get somewhere, holding a door open for someone or letting them go before you is akin to raising a public nuisance. In a crowd of people you wouldn't be considered a "gentleman" as you might elsewhere in the world. "Fend for yourself," my *sifu* said in a matter-of-fact tone. I didn't fully understand it at the time, but I knew he knew what he was talking about. It took some getting used to.

Although the women in Hong Kong, as well as Japan, enjoy parallels with men in terms of social and work environments in large cities, the Chinese and Japanese societies as a whole are still very male-dominated.

While in Hong Kong we trained in wing chun under Ip Ching. Amazingly, Ip Ching was one of two sons of Ip Man—Bruce Lee's first teacher! Just the thought of that sent shivers up my spine and gave me renewed focus. In some strange indirect way, I was being touched by Bruce Lee himself and felt a connection.

My discomfort was unrelenting and escalated even further when I became sick with a flu and fever. Ip Ching helped to relieve my fear, taking me to a hospital for help. Healthcare in Hong Kong is exemplary; their citizens enjoy the fifth longest life expectancy in the world as well as the fifth lowest rate of infant mortality. By comparison, the United States is rated as the fiftieth. This fact surprises many people who have never travelled to Hong Kong and confuse its crowded shores and multinational citizenry as being behind the times.

Once we arrived at the kung fu school, I saw that it did not have the traditional American set up with an entrance, gear shop, nice vibrant training floor, etc. It was a simple building. The décor was fairly basic. The students didn't wear "kung fu" uniforms. Not only was it much smaller than most, but when we had class training, everyone there simply wore their ordinary street clothes. It was strange watching martial artists work out wearing jeans and polo shirts. For most people who are brought up in the streets of Asia, wearing some strange outfit when learning how to fight just wasn't realistic for them. I suppose that made sense on some level.

We also trained in judo under my *sensei*, Kong Chan's, father. He was the former coach of the Hong Kong Olympic judo team, so it was quite an honor. I was impressed at how we were welcomed with open arms. I was equally impressed that all of the father's children wore black belts and had studied from a very young age.

I was *really* homesick. I missed not only my parents, but also the comfort food of home. When a wave of homesickness overtook me, I headed to the closest McDonald's and buried myself in pancakes and Chicken McNuggets™. I had also just decided to become a quasi-vegetarian, eating no meat except chicken. I didn't eat beef or pork. A lot of Chinese food has pork in it. So, in times like this, I just ate white rice. China is the world's largest producer of rice. I drank Coke™ and water mainly, too young to drink alcohol. I also liked the various Chinese herbal teas that came with some of the food. Even though these are referred to as teas, there is generally no tea in them at all. These bitter or lightly sweet drinks are made solely from herbs and supposedly are able to cure a great many diseases. Served cool, they are often consumed to relieve the overwhelming heat and humidity of the city.

Hong Kong had a unique scent; it even smelled different than the States. While there we ate out a lot, visiting all the food stalls and small restaurants frequented by the locals. Much of their food is presented and sold in old-world style open markets where much of the fare you eat is slaughtered and cured right before your eyes. It was quite unnerving walking by a pork stand where freshly slaughtered pigs hung on hooks as the advertisement. For me that wasn't an inducement to eat, but a deterrent!

I'm sure that based on my first visit to Hong Kong, not feeling very well and frowning at some of the food, none of my training partners there would have ever imagined that someday I would actually choose to live in Asia. Being underestimated was beginning to become a kind of theme for me.

As Americans, we are accustomed to eating with utensils: knives, forks and spoons. But as we've all seen in the movies, most people in Asia eat with chopsticks. You can still use forks and spoons in most of the restaurants, but not so if you plan on eating at street stalls, old-world style.

As in most countries in the Far East and Europe, shopping was always done through negotiations rather than simply checking the price on the tag and then paying for the merchandise. In Hong Kong, bargaining wasn't just a process but an art form that they took very seriously.

Our two weeks in Hong Kong came to an end and it was finally time to leave this enchanted place and return home. One of the things I found myself regretting a little was not being more open-minded in trying more of their foods. Some of the food that I did try, I loved; food like *dim sum* which I tried earnestly to find in local Chinese restaurants when I arrived home.

Chinese food in America isn't authentic; meaning many

31

of the dishes served at restaurants in America are not on the menus in Hong Kong. *Dim sum* is a wonderful Chinese dish comprised of small steamed or fried savory dumplings packed with various fillings and served as a snack or the main course.

As you can imagine it didn't take long for me to start planning my return trip. I was hooked on the people, the culture and the land, and it was where I wanted to live someday.

Chapter Six

My Japanese Horizon

After my trip to Hong Kong I knew exactly what I wanted out of life and where I intended to spend it. The speculation about my future was so distracting that I completely lost interest in school and stopped doing homework altogether.

Shortly after my return, I walked into my counselor's office with a whole new resolve and vigor. Ordinarily, school administrative offices were not my favorite places, but I was on a mission and this was just the first of many doors I would open to achieve what I wanted. I had given the options a lot of thought and come up with a plan; to ask about studying abroad. I wasn't sure exactly how that worked, or if it was even possible for me, but I knew that the life that awaited me in Grand Rapids was not enough; I wanted more. Originally I wanted to study abroad in Hong Kong. After my visit, I realized I loved everything about it, but there were more options that beckoned. *What about Thailand or Japan*?

Hong Kong is a very, very old civilization and has withstood highly varied governments. It became a part of China's Qin Dynasty in 221 BC and it is believed that salt production was a major economic contribution. In the 19th century, the British government relied heavily on China for tea and when the Chinese demanded silver imports in return and the British supply could not supply the demand, the British instead supplied the Chinese market with opium. At that time, opium was legal in Britain. The Chinese were not happy about this trade arrangement and entered into the First Opium War with the British in 1800s. The ensuing British victory included occupation of Hong Kong.

When Hong Kong was later returned to China in 1997 after the British colonization ended, many of the existing businesses left. This made the choices I had in Hong Kong very limited. The school I had planned to study with was one of those companies that left, so I thought either Japan or Thailand could be a better choice. I think, in looking back, due to my mother's bi-polar condition and how I dealt with it, there was always a strong motivation to leave home. There was no question that I loved her, but anyone who has lived with someone who is bi-polar will understand when I say that it's a challenging and insecure way of life. The mood swings and erratic behavior that the condition causes make it difficult to have family continuity. So many plans must revolve around the illness, as it shows no respect for commitment.

It turned out that my parents were actually open to the idea of my studying abroad and since Hong Kong was no longer a practical option, the choice of Thailand or Japan weighed heavily on my mind. Thailand was a consideration because I wanted to learn muay thai kickboxing; and Japan because I wanted to learn more judo. My parents felt Japan would be the best choice because it was known to be a safer place to live. So it came about that my new life would begin in Japan.

Unfortunately, I discovered (although this was not necessarily a surprise considering the fact that I had stopped applying myself) that I didn't have the grades to study abroad in Japan. There was a minimum GPA required and mine was too low. This is especially true regarding the minimum GPA required to study abroad in Japan due to the strength of its academic system. That's when I took things into my own hands again. I asked my counselor whether I might find a language school instead of studying abroad in the traditional way, at a high school. Thus ensued a great deal of research at a local bookstore on the subject. Once I figured out how to make an international phone call, I even called the Japanese language school directly. After speaking with them, I immediately applied and, thankfully, was accepted.

I visited my counselor again to see if I could study abroad for my final high school semester. To my relief, he said I could, indeed, study abroad the way I had suggested.

For this to happen, however, I would need to improve my current grades, but that would not be a problem for the "rejuvenated" me. Once I heard these simple terms, I immediately found the motivation necessary and soon raised my GPA to a perfect 4.0. I would be awarded the remaining semester high school credit for studying Japanese in Japan.

Once my family and I were certain that I was going to study in Japan, we began to do some more serious research. My mother mentioned my plans to a clerk in a local fabric store in Grand Rapids where she frequently shopped. Reuben had relatives living in Japan and she felt he might be able to give me some valuable advice.

It just so happened that Reuben's brother, David, lived in Yokohama City - Kanagawa Prefecture, about 20 miles south of Tokyo. After speaking with them we were able to arrange for his brother, David and his wife, Gloria, to pick me up at the airport, so everything was set. My maternal grandfather offered to subsidize my first six months in the school. I was, indeed, privileged.

~

My nerves created butterflies the size of eagles in my stomach. Was I really ready for this?

~

My nerves on the morning of my flight to Japan were so great that the butterflies in my stomach seemed the size of eagles. I was constantly re-assessing my decision to study abroad and it was driving me crazy. *Was I really ready for this?* I would ask myself over and over again, *or was I just kidding myself?*

Once the airplane took off and I could see the buildings and Earth below shrink to the size of small toys, I realized there was no turning back and my choice would stand – for better or for worse.

On the plane, crossing the Pacific Ocean I think the people sitting next to me noticed how tense I was. Prior to landing, a video played showing the process of going through customs. I must have looked confused.

The man sitting next to me was named Patrick. He was originally from America. Patrick was slim and of average height, accompanied by his Japanese wife who had shining black hair that fell just past her shoulders. They lived in Tokyo and calmed me down by explaining the process of entering Japan.

The plan was simple. I would be in Japan for six months. At the time I knew nothing about visas and how it would affect my ability to stay in Japan legally, but I was about to learn the hard way. I would learn later that Americans were allowed to stay in Japan using a 90-day tourist visa. That visa would be issued by customs. I also discovered that students who planned to study in Japan or stay longer than the ninety days usually received a student's visa with the help of the school they attended. At the time I didn't know any of this and had been told to visit a neighboring country for a few days before returning to Japan to receive a new ninety-day tourist visa. There was so much I still needed to learn.

Japan is one of dozens of countries that participate in the Visa Waiver Program (VWP) that allows nationals of certain countries to travel to the U.S. for 90 days or less for the purpose of tourism or business without actually obtaining a conventional visa.

Patrick actually led me to the customs line. I remember him listening to a loudspeaker announcement in Japanese and interpreting it for me. I couldn't help but think, *hopefully, I will be able to understand that for myself one day...* I never saw Patrick and his wife again. We spoke once or twice by phone while I was in the Japanese school but that was it. Unfortunately, we lost touch.

When the custom's officer asked me how long I was planning to stay, I foolishly told them "six months." I was very matter of fact when I explained my plan to just leave after 90 days and then return for another visa. They quickly ushered me off to a back room, and that's when I really started to worry. The room was sterile in appearance and I felt like a fly under a microscope. I could feel the panic rising in my throat as I considered my situation and ignorance of how their system worked. My palms were sweating and my face flushed with fear. I didn't know what was going on or where they were taking me. I wasn't sure at that point what my crime was. I knew I was a good person, so why all the hostility?

The officers started barking at me with questions about my intentions in Japan. Apparently they thought I was up to no good; trying to do something illegal. They told me they were prepared to put me on a flight back to America immediately. There was a lot of innuendo and complicated dialogue for a young seventeen-year-old to handle. My head spun and my mind raced to all sorts of strange outcomes. Was I about to be thrown into some Japanese prison or shackled and sent back to the States? Frightened and all alone, I believed the world was about to end for me right there in that room!

I pleaded with them for over an hour, begging them to believe my story, frantically reassuring them that I didn't have an evil plan and wasn't a threat. Just when all hope seemed lost, one of the guards seemed to be buying my story. It's possible the whole thing was an act because I was a young foreigner, but if it was an act they should have clearly been given an Academy Award. After much more desperate pleading, they finally believed my story and permitted me to enter their country. *Talk about a warm welcome!* I thought, ruing the stark difference between the smiley-faced airport posters and the bizarre reality.

Thankfully, the day's events progressed more smoothly from there. David and Gloria duly picked me up with their car and I can remember that ride like it was yesterday. I was much calmer now and ate the atmosphere with a hunger of excitement. I wanted to appreciate everything I could absorb about my new home.

Every country has its own smell and ambiance and Japan is no different. With Japan it's a slight scent of cigarette smoke mingled with food and concrete. The cigarette smoke is thick in the stale air because so many people smoke. It's an odd, but distinct, odor. The Japanese government controls tobacco companies and has few anti-smoking laws; enabling the Japanese to be consumers of over 350 billion cigarettes each year with low-taxed, inexpensive government-supported sources.

Once on the highway I remember looking out the window on our drive from Narita City in Chiba Prefecture, past Tokyo, down to Yokohama.

I could see bright neon lights from stores and billboards in the background as we passed through Tokyo. It was obvious that the city was cutting edge of electronic technology. This had not always been the case. Other Asian countries were rivals in the gadgets market and their prices were more competitive. Tokyo managed to regain the advantage through one product in particular; televisions.

I was looking forward to getting my hands on some of the electronic toys. The United States was, at that time, far behind the curve that Tokyoites enjoyed. Emailing by cell phone was not possible in the U.S., while it had already become the norm in Tokyo. Phones literally spilled off the shelves here in a myriad of colors and patterns. They were able to broadcast television, included step-by-step GPS, play music and there was a version with large keys intended for seniors.

I stayed with David and his wife for a week at their home in the Negishi district of Yokohama City - Kanagawa Prefecture. While there, I spent much of my time sightseeing and trying new foods. These were both new worlds to me and my curiosity propelled me to try everything at least once. David took me to a local ramen shop and this was the first time I tried it. Growing up, I had eaten ramen noodles often, but this was different and quite delicious. Traditionally, the soup is made from chicken or pork stock, which meant my options were limited. The restaurant was small and in a back alley off a main road. David was obviously a regular, as the ramen chef knew him by name. As we took a seat at the counter, David introduced me. I took David's advice and ordered the miso ramen. Miso is a traditional Japanese seasoning, produced by fermenting rice, barley and/or soybeans with salt and the fungus kōjikin. The most typical miso is made with soy. The noodles were hand-made in house and were amazing. In Japan, slurping is not considered bad manners, and I did my share that night. It was delicious.

My stay with David and his wife was memorable in many ways. One day while David was at work, I accompanied Gloria while she ran some errands. We were at a mall near the Yokosuka Navy Base where David worked. I remember getting on an elevator and being shocked by all the people on one small escalator. Gloria taught me how to say, "excuse me" as we got off the elevator saying "*sumimasen... sumimasen...*"

The second week they dropped me off at Shibusawa Kokusai Gakuen, the Japanese language school that I would be attending. It was located in the countryside of a prefecture called Saitama, just north of Tokyo. Here was where I would spend the first six months studying and learning the Japanese language. A prefecture is more like a state than a city because it's much larger and more populated.

On the night of my arrival it was deadly silent. The quiet was very different from the vibrant city of Yokohama where I had been staying with David and his wife. With the exception of one person waiting for me to arrive, there wasn't another soul around for miles. I wouldn't meet any of the other students until class began on the following day. It was a bit intimidating and certainly very different from my home back in the States.

Although it was isolated, the school grounds were actually very nice and spacious compared to big cities like Yokohama or Tokyo. It had stand-alone dormitory housing; a few small apartments that students who wanted their own space could rent. It had a Koi pond by the *shokudo,* or cafeteria.

I spent eight hours a day in a school that seemed incredibly isolated, shrouded in silence. I don't think I fully appreciated the peaceful aspect of that silence—so different from the larger cities of the Orient and even of my hometown back in Michigan. The school was located in the city of Fukaya, about two hours from Tokyo and 3.5 or 4 hours from Yokohama. I lived in a dormitory on the school grounds where we were provided with breakfast, lunch and dinner by the school. Breakfast might be cereal and toast or fish and rice. Lunch provided a bit more variety—Japanese curry was my favorite. Other options included pasta, pizza and other more recognizable choices.

The school was very different from U.S. high schools. It catered to adults. We wore slippers inside the classrooms and its design was spartan by comparison.

Construction objectives in Japan are very different from many countries in North America and Europe. Buildings are expected to have a much shorter lifespan. Indeed, concrete buildings have an intended life of only three decades. Old Japanese buildings are poorly heated, so many rooms contained portable propane heaters. After a long class, the smell could become quite overwhelming and even make you a little dizzy.

I met two other Americans during the semester I was there, but I didn't spend much time with them, as they were much older than I was. I compared this environment to my experience in Hong Kong. I was a bit older this time and things were being seen from a whole new perspective. Suddenly I was seeing everything with new eyes and hearing everything with new ears. I'm not sure if it was my age; perhaps I was just becoming more open to change, but things really did seem different this time. It's amazing what a couple years can do to a young man's perspective about people and places.

One thing I found fascinating was that compared to the cities, life moved much slower in the countryside. It took some getting used when the locals tended to stare at us *gaijin* (foreigners) because it was rare to find us visiting their communities. This added attention might make some people feel special, but I found it made me feel uncomfortable at times.

A strong sense of animosity between Americans and Japanese still exists even today. While WWII took place over 70 years ago, much of the resulting destruction and loss of life took place on Japanese soil with the bombing of Hiroshima and Nagasaki. Two months after the bombing of Pearl Harbor by the Japanese, President Roosevelt signed Executive Order 9066 that placed 122,000 Japanese Americans into relocation camps. This order did not include those living in Hawaii, as they comprised over 40% of the Hawaiian population and thus workforce, making it unfeasible. The Japanese people enjoy a long and binding history of which tradition forms the foundation. While the major cities have leapt forward with technology and a more global sense of participation, much of the countryside tends to look backward and treasure tradition. Typically their lives do not include foreigners, no matter the nationality.

At first, I tended to just smile or nod; perhaps I would try to offer a brief wave. Some people tended to look away, either in humility or indifference. Others would nod or bow in return and say *konnichiwa* (good afternoon).

Nevertheless, I found myself learning so much about this beautiful country. The houses were bigger outside the cities and often housed older people in their 60s and 70s. Japan is an aging country; one where time seems almost suspended.

In an age where societies all over the world are encouraged to be competitive and transparent, this seemed to be a place that time forgot. People here were not concerned with the outside world; they tended to their own quiet lives in a very basic way. One of the things I found unusual was people burned all their raw trash right in their front yards to get rid of it. While "foul" might be too strong a word, the smells these piles emanated certainly had a potent fragrance. It was noticeable, but not horrific. It permeated my life there in one way or another.

Larger cities in Japan offered commuter trains to transport the larger populations. By contrast, those in the countryside drove cars or rode bicycles. I used the train on days I'd like to adventure out and see the nearby areas. The train station was a 30-minute bike ride away. Consequently I spent much of my time simply pushing the pedals. The trains offered a welcomed relief and were world-class in design. In general, train travel was comfortable and hassle-free, although in my case it carried a unique rejection. It was not uncommon for fellow riders to assess me and then go to lengths not to sit next to me. Older Japanese men and women alike often disliked foreigners and I obviously did not fit in with their societal expectations. I could feel their disapproving stares. In hindsight, I wish I'd known that this was due in part to my *foreignness* or *FOB*, "fresh off the boat" aura surrounding me. As time passed and I had begun to adapt to Japan, I found this happened less and less as years went by; particularly as my body language started to resemble theirs, meaning losing the "lost" look, more subtle movements, etc.

It wasn't long before I began missing my car. In the U.S., with the exception of some major cities, it is almost impossible to work and lead a normal life, particularly as a young man, without an automobile.

Americans tend to view public transportation as the poor man's solution. In Japan, however, the public transportation was a vast improvement and very useful. It was not uncommon to sit next to doctors and lawyers on a bus or a train; there is no negative connotation with public transportation. It is quite common for Japanese to live outside the large cities yet commute to their city jobs. These transports are solidly packed, many passengers standing throughout the trip and donning surgical masks to avoid germ contamination between one another. I actually eventually grew to prefer commuting by train instead of by car. To this day I miss the public transportation in Japan. I wonder if the Midwestern stigma will ever change.

Of all the new experiences, my real frustration came from a lack of speaking the language. Unlike English, French, German and Spanish which are all Latin-based languages, there was nothing even vaguely familiar in the phrases I heard about me. The cadence was especially foreign, so it was difficult to relate intonation to even the most basic of responses. Japanese isn't a tonal language and is what makes it one of the world's most difficult languages to learn. Unlike Latin languages which one can usually learn to "read" by sounding them out, Japanese made me feel illiterate at the outset and it would take a long time before I became accustomed to it.

From the moment I arrived, my command of the Japanese language was very, very limited. As a result, I felt isolated and alone most of the time. Sometimes the anxiety was so great that I would even lock myself in my room to avoid having to expose my broken Japanese to the locals. The result was overwhelming and on more than one occasion, brought me to tears.

Thus, I found myself again questioning my decision to follow through on this commitment. Sometimes there is greater wisdom in realizing that you've made an error in decision and be willing to take a step back. For me, however, it was too late for that. I was still just a young man in a foreign land. No matter how much I loved it or the rationale I would use to prop up my homesickness, I often still harbored self-doubts. I didn't even know how to shave yet and I certainly couldn't cook. My scenario clearly had the potential for disaster.

When I found myself filled with doubts, I looked back to the reason I had come to Japan in the first place. I was not here as a tourist; not here because incautious parents were spoiling me. I reminded myself that I had come to learn to fight. This was a quest to overcome so many obstacles. I asked myself whether I was ready to give up before I even gave it a chance. I decided I was not. I was in Japan to stay… at least until I accomplished what I had come here to do.

Chapter Seven

The Lessons Begin

The classroom environment was intense. The Japanese put a lot of stock in education.

In retrospect, I am grateful to have had that classroom structure. There is a major difference between learning a foreign language in a traditional classroom and learning through total immersion. Using the necessity of learning a language in order to function is the best way to achieve true fluency. We were expected to only speak in Japanese from the first day, so there was an added pressure; but an effective one. Textbooks were not in English. This meant that to move forward you were absolutely forced to interpret them.

We spent the first week learning the two basic Japanese alphabets, *hiragana* and *katakana*, and relatively speaking, that was the easy stuff. Beginning week two, we were expected to read and write Japanese daily. We used it in class all the time. We would also eventually learn *kanji*, or hieroglyphic-style characters that originated in the Chinese language.

Despite living in a dormitory filled with students from all over the world, I still felt isolated. I needed to shift my focus away from my discomfort and challenges, and back on my martial arts. That's what I did. Whenever I found myself with open time, I would meet with an older Japanese judo coach who would take me down to the local high school to train with their team. I also practiced judo every Sunday at the local police station. This was made possible thanks to Shibusawa Kokusai Gakuen, my language school. They set it all up for me by contacting both the judo coach as well as the local police office. This really helped me to forget what I didn't know or couldn't do, and focus more on the things I

45

wanted to do; the things I did know as well as improve my skills at fighting.

Judo was created by Jigoro Kano. What many people may not realize is that the sport is more about competitive manipulation and not swinging at your opponent with your hands and feet. The idea is to throw or takedown your opponent—immobilizing him with strategy. In many ways this sport reflects a common Japanese lifestyle; to live in harmonious appreciation with your elements and not to fight them. To triumph means that you respect your opponent but learn to control the situation with a minimum of violence and a maximum of harmony.

As the practices began, I was really nervous. Judo rooms have a distinct smell; similar to a wrestling room or a school gymnasium with mats on the floor. It's a mixture of wood, vinyl mats and the sweat of innumerable hard practices. Many people don't realize it, but judo is the second most-practiced sport in the world. It has gained popularity since its inception in 1882. It's extremely popular in Japan as a martial art and sport; it has been so for centuries.

I worked very hard during my stay in Japan. I learned every thing possible and practiced my skills each and every day. By the time I returned to the U.S. I had earned my first degree black belt, *shodan*, in judo. Even more honorably, it was earned from the Kodokan, the International Headquarters of Judo in the center of Tokyo. What I took most pride in was the fact that I had earned by black belt in Japan, rather than in the U.S. and the sheer lengths I had to go to in order to accomplish that.

In America, a student of judo needed to be able to perform several throws properly and they also needed to be able to do *nage-no-kata*, a pre-determined set of throws. In Japan you earned your black belt by competing in an event that was more like a state college championship wrestling tournament. It was an interesting, daunting difference.

On weekends when I wasn't studying or training in judo, I travelled to Tokyo by train to get lost in the city and really see the place. I had never ventured out on my own before in a city of this size. There were so many people and everything moved so fast. I spent most of my time people-watching and just trying to take everything in.

One weekend, I found my way to the headquarters of judo, The Kodokan. The building was massive, not your ordinary martial arts school. It had to be big to house the practitioners who traveled from all over the world to learn the art of judo. Watching them practice helped remind me of how far I had come.

People and their culture were very different on this side of the globe and in the coming years, I was be able to confirm just how different. Not only did they *do* things differently, they *thought* differently as well. That would become more apparent with each month I spent there. Outside of school, I was usually the only foreigner and the day I tested for my *shodan* would be no different. I could feel everyone's eyes on me. I felt completely uncomfortable as they treated me as though I was an oddity. It was a feeling I would learn to endure. I wished I could magically blend in with everybody else. I know that everybody often wondered what the *gaijin* was doing there. Was he good enough—strong enough? Could I measure up?

The test was held at two different times. The first session covered levels of 3-kyuu, 2-kyuu and 1-kyuu; levels one through three at the brown-belt level. I competed in fifteen matches on the same day and won them all. This was no small feat and I felt an immense sense of pride in my own accomplishment.

The second test was for *shodan*, which is for the 1st-degree black belt. On that particular day I competed in five different matches and won all five of them. Clearly I had overcome my obstacles and had now achieved two of my life-long goals; to earn my black belt in Japan and to learn a foreign language. All my hard work was paying off and, better still, the cyst in my brain seemed to be cooperating. For the first time in an age, I felt happy, hopeful and motivated about my life. More over, I felt a sense of accomplishment and pride that I had chosen the harder path and endured. I was doing something most just dream about, and doing it well.

Although I graduated from high school, I decided not to attend the graduation ceremony. At this point, high school was no longer a priority for me. My sense of achievement and the milestones by which I would judge my life had separated from a mere grade school progression. I felt like I was finally free to travel my path. I chose, instead, to spend those last few days in Japan. I had finally begun to understand some of the language so I wanted to stay as long as possible so that I could continue to practice and improve.

That fall of '97 found me once again in Grand Rapids, anticipating my entry to college. I chose to attend Friend's World Program, offered through Long Island University. This was considered an experiential education, providing an international experience that would result in a liberal arts education. Its now called Global College. This was an expensive choice and it was necessary to obtain school loans. This was later a major factor in my choice to drop out after the first year.

Looking back over my initial time spent in Japan, I realized that as difficult as it had been, with its rigid culture and indifferent acceptance, I was still determined to make it work. Despite its obstacles, I had learned to like many special things about that country that set it apart.

One unexpected discovery was that the more I tried it, the more I discovered that the food was an adventure. Sushi is amazing. I realize for many people, the thought of eating raw fish is unappetizing. But, trust me, after you try it, you might just change your mind! Sushi chefs take their trade very seriously. Each piece is made with perfection.

Then, there was the specialized martial arts training to consider; something that I could receive only in Japan.

The younger generation of Japanese liked Americans and were much more tolerant and open-minded. They found anything American desirable from movies to music to manufactured products and fads. In some sense, that also included me.

I had fallen in love with the country more each day. I liked to think that perhaps some day they would accept me as one of their own. That was what I truly yearned for. Clearly, I still had a lot to learn and my understanding would come slowly. I had already accomplished so much at a young age and was sure that nothing could stop me from realizing all my dreams and goals.

The cyst couldn't stop me. The Japanese culture couldn't slow me down. Not even my immaturity could convince me to give up. For me the sky was the limit and I felt like flying. As the saying goes, however, everything that goes up must come down. My crash was yet to come.

Chapter Eight

Culture Shock

It was the time in my life when guys my age were headed off to college. For many, this meant the first time away from home; flying the coop, being a real adult and all that entails. When other mothers were packing footlockers with extra underwear and socks, I found that all seemed so tame. I had already seen so much, travelled so far and made so many hard decisions, college presented no challenge. Furthermore, I thought of it as a means to an end and a successful career in martial arts was the end I had in mind.

Nevertheless, I had journeyed to New York to attend college as well as study more Japanese. I hoped that all the time I was dedicating to learning the language would make a huge difference this time. It was important that I fit in with the Japanese and having a better command of their language would go a long way toward that.

I found college lacking. I expected more from it. It bothered me that the other students seemed so content to simply drink and party their way through; apparently oblivious to all the advantages a higher education would bring. I had no interest in that kind of bedlam and was almost disgusted by their lack of serious drive and the wasted opportunities. Perhaps they were too young to understand goals yet. I felt so much older than my years.

On the other hand, I knew exactly what I wanted out of life; it was much more than a few parties and superficial fun. Much more. I had big goals and aspirations that were very important to me and what was more important, I knew the path to my success.

In January of 1998 I traveled back to Japan for the second time. I was pretty naïve about a lot of things back then and would speak openly about my desire to someday become a professional mixed martial artist. I truly believed it would happen if only I would stay focused and work hard.

I stayed again with David and his wife in their home back in Yokohama, Japan and I really enjoyed our time together. David was an African-American and his wife, Gloria, was Filipina. While David's primary career was in the Navy, he had worked in the photography field for many years and even had a small related business that brought in some extra cash. He and Gloria took pictures at weddings and banquets, helping whomever needed his services. It paid the bills and put food on the table. I learned an important lesson about combining your work and income with something that you actually love doing in life. Sometimes that's more important than anything else, and more often than not—it's where you will be the happiest and most successful.

I had planned to rent a small room from David and Gloria for at least six months but after only two, I decided it was time to move out. They lived in a two-bedroom condo with the bedrooms upstairs and the kitchen, dining, and living rooms were on the main floor. Naval base housing is nice; a spacious condo-type building similar to what we have in West Michigan. It was definitely a lot bigger than anything I could have rented.

* * * * *

Japan is one of America's closest allies, yet this relationship is threatened.

The U.S. military presence in Japan is viewed by some as protection against hostile neighbors such as North Korea. Others feel that the presence of America and its bases on Japanese soil could be the exact opposite; a reason for an attack. As neighboring countries, Korean and Japanese histories are deep. In Japan, it is common knowledge that the two harbor harsh feelings for one another. This dates back to WWII when Japan occupied Korea. Located near one another, their history of interaction is very long and complicated. In early history, Japan owed much, but not all, of its cultural heritage to Korea. During the 15th and 16 centuries, when Japan was unified after centuries of civil war, Japan relentlessly invaded Korea. This was the last large-scale conquest campaign that Korea suffered until the 20th century. In the early 20th century, Japan once again invaded Korea, annexed it, and committed atrocities that rivaled the Holocaust. After the war, many Japanese leaders would continue to pay tribute to the war criminals of WWII, claiming that Japanese Imperialism was beneficial to the invaded countries, and denied the existence of their atrocities.

Modern relations between Korea and Japan is so egregiously bad, both Koreans and Japanese tend to learn the points of the history in school that make themselves feel superior and vilify one another. To make matters worse, North Korea has regularly threatened to launch missile attacks on Japan.

Furthermore, the persistent American saber rattling with North Korea worries the Japanese, especially those living near American military bases that are prime targets should North Korea decide to strike, or ideal retaliatory targets should the U.S. decide to bomb North Korea.

Another source of friction is that Japan has a very low crime rate and the presence of thousands of young American GIs result in numerous robberies, assaults, rapes, and murders of Japanese citizens each year. This has given America and Americans in Japan a bad reputation. At the time, I thought that being fully accepted by the Japanese would ultimately lead to success in Japan and help me avoid many of the hurdles that I would need to face as a foreigner.

The average Japanese has very little opportunity to interact with gaijin (foreigners) as a whole, and even less with Black Americans.

Oversimplifying a complex topic, Americans enjoy a lowly opinion, and the lowest of these are Black Americans. That said, they still rank above Black Africans. I use the term "Black Americans" specifically because "African American" is a term used generally in the United States, but rarely elsewhere. Those on the continent of Africa don't even recognize the term "African American." The Japanese are intrigued by Black American culture but many are hesitant to approach us, much less befriend us. It was important to me to do my part to try and change the way we were perceived. I did not want to contribute to any act or participation that would reflect adversely on my country or ethnicity.

David and Gloria were not involved in any of that unsavory business either, but it was still all around us. Living on the base and being on hand through the weekends made it impossible to avoid. It came time to experience life in Japan on my own; away from the influence of a military base, or those "contributing to this negativity". I wanted to experience the "real" Japan alone and I couldn't really do that living there.

I have a tendency to be a homebody when I'm not training, even today. Perhaps this is because I've traveled so much and therefore look forward to being at home. On weekends I occasionally accompanied David when he went out. He persisted in trying to get me out into the public and to meet people. He and I went to a hip-hop club named "Charlie's" a few times on the weekends. It was located across the street from a popular park in Yokohama, *Yamashita Koen*, or Yamashita Park. He did their flyer design work and handled occasional photo shoots there from time to time. It was a popular hangout for the younger military crowd.

I appreciated David's efforts to get me involved in a social life, but this sort of fun just didn't hold a great deal of appeal for me. It was the same sort of feeling I got from the university back home in the States; this felt contrived and careless. Perhaps I was extraordinarily serious, and yes, maybe even boring by the standards of that time, age and place in the world. Then again, perhaps it had something to do with the fact that my brain held a stick of dynamite that could ignite at any time and I did not want to fritter away life.

There is a logic that holds that when you are young, you have the greatest potential to absorb, plan, achieve and set your life's course. If that time is spent drinking, smoking, drugging and engaging in meaningless sex – as many young people tend to do, then it stands to reason you have not only set that same path for your future, but have compromised the advantages that youth affords.

I didn't drink alcohol at the time; nor did I smoke. Clubs in Japan are ecosystems of smoke. They are dimly lit with a minimum of lights and generally employ DJs who toll loud music to lure patrons on the dance floor. It is a world where young guys attempt to seduce young girls and the result is often a night best forgotten, but often repeated.

Next door was a convenience store named Family Mart. It was not unusual for young men on high-powered mopeds to loudly buzz the traffic and pedestrians along this busy street. They challenged drivers and invited violence; defying any police attempts to banish them. I would learn later that they were part of a gang called *"Kanto Rengo-kai Bosozoku" or "Kanto Rengo" for short.* The *Bosozoku Biker* gang was often involved in brawls and fights, in and outside these clubs. Those who looked as if they were athletic or tough were commonly targeted and challenged.

This world was not for me. I had not come this far to haunt booze-slopped floors and lose myself amongst this superficial multitude. All I wanted to do was train. Staying healthy enough to fight professionally was a very serious business for me.

It was not the easiest of accomplishments, but by March of 1998 I found myself a place to live in the *Ishikawacho* district of Yokohama City. I remember the day I went to inspect the room for the first time. To say that it was less than ideal would be an understatement. The place was small, dingy and dirty. This was not the way I had been brought up and certainly not how I saw my future. I had mixed feelings about it and was hesitant at first, but there were no other options presenting themselves. I told myself that living conditions were not why I had come back to Japan and that a bit of adversity could only make me stronger and more determined to succeed. So, I moved in.

It was what was known as a *gaijin house*, which simply meant a foreigner's house. The Japanese are a discriminating peoples and this trait is considered almost honorable. Their prejudice ranges from annoyance to disgust to outright non-acknowledgement and its basis depends on a variety of factors. But one thing is consistent; irrespective of race or background, and because the real estate market is so different in Japan, these *gaijin houses* were just considered more suited for foreigners. If you weren't Japanese, you were considered a foreigner – at least according to many Japanese landlords. Perhaps tolerance would be a better description of how foreigners were looked upon. One reason for this lay in that sometimes foreigners renting, or even purchasing, a home would leave the country without paying their bills. When this happened, the landlord was unable to collect his due and thus absorbed the loss. The few dishonest foreigners made it very difficult for those who paid their bills.

My new home away from home rented for 45,000 *yen*, or about $450.00 U.S. per month. In a country of such serene beauty, the bedding I received was dirty; obviously unwashed in years. I remember another tenant living there had to be treated for *dani*, or bedbug bites all over her body.

I shared a window with a Nepalese couple crammed into the room right next to mine. Since our rooms shared the window, my room often smelled like the Nepalese curry they used to eat in their room. In retrospect, I had to commend them. They had come to work in Japan to give their family a better life in Nepal. They had only made 900 yen an hour ($9.00 an hour U.S.) but that went much further in Nepal. They sent it home to provide their children with an education.

I was given a futon, a type of traditional sleeping mat that lay flat upon the floor. This was not the convertible sofa that Americans normally would expect. It clearly had never been washed. A four-minute shower was an additional 100 yen ($1.00 U.S.) and again, this was not how I had been brought up. I would often fill buckets of water at the sink, soap myself, and rinse off using my bucket of water to avoid paying the extra money. The bathroom was a communal area along with the kitchen, so everybody in the building shared these.

You might wonder why I was so attracted to Japan when it was so unfriendly for Americans. Mixed martial arts were illegal in most of the states in the U.S. Where it was legal, my weight class wasn't recognized. In Japan, I didn't have that problem, so the obvious choice was to suffer a bit in order to learn my craft.

Shortly after renting the room, I found a job as a barista at a local business called *Seattle Café,* located in the Cial shopping center inside the Yokohama train station. It was a reasonable ride by train from Ishikawacho to the *gaijin house* where I lived.

It was always curious to me that while Americans were considered lowly, anything American was trendy and popular, including coffee houses in a land where most people drank tea. I made about 90,000 yen or $900 per month. Needless to say, splurging for me was literally a trip to McDonald's.

Working at Seattle Café served two purposes. Not only was it a way to make a living, but more importantly I was working in a Japanese environment that could help me continue to learn the language. Sometimes the smallest of actions can make all the difference in the world.

It was at the Seattle Café that I learned one more lesson in Japanese etiquette. One day a customer came in and ordered a milkshake. I quickly made it, placed the straw in it and went to hand it to the customer. My boss suddenly snatched it out of my hand and quickly tilted the straw to the side, apologizing to the customer as he handed it to him. I was taken aback and didn't understand the problem. I then learned that in Japan, placing chopsticks, or in this case a straw, straight up is inconsiderate, and may even be considered some sort of curse.

Apparently standing chopsticks upright was tantamount to a death curse, mirroring as it did the image of an upright grave marker at a cemetery. The same applied to passing food back and forth chopstick to chopstick. Using these two small sticks must be monitored closely. At traditional funerals it was customary to place a bowl of rice on the altar with chopsticks standing straight up. It's also customary to pass bones, retrieved from a cremation, from chopstick to chopstick. Doing it correctly was crucial.

This was only one example of a multitude of customs and rules that must be observed in Japan. Foreigners commonly misunderstand them, so even working in a Japanese environment provided valuable lessons. It was one of the best ways for me to improve my Japanese fluency and learn the culture.

I worked hard every day at my new job and any time I had left over was spent searching for a gym suitable for my training. That was, after all, the whole reason I had come to Japan.

Chapter Nine

The Warrior

Once I was settled into my new home and job at the café, I began my search for the right gym where I could pursue the training I had come for. It took some time but one day after work I finally found such a place. While flipping through some magazines at a bookstore in my neighborhood, I came across a magazine called *Kakutougi Tsushiin*. Inside, I found a list of various mixed martial arts organizations in the area. I knew that the sport had been banned in many states in the U.S. and learned that many of the best fighters in the world actually competed in Japan in an organization known as *Shooto*.

To my elation there was actually a telephone number listed, although I didn't dare hope it would still be valid. Nevertheless, I called and got the headquarters. In my best (broken) Japanese, I asked if there was a gym near me in Yokohama. Again to my delight, the voice on the line confirmed that there was.

The very next day I found my way to *Shooting Gym Yokohama* and quickly headed inside to check it out for myself. The term "shooting" refers to the style of fighting. "Shooting" or "shoot fighting" was derived from and based on the principals of boxing, muay thai kickboxing and catch wrestling. Catch wrestling is similar to Brazilian jiu-jitsu but focuses more on the flow of one submission to the next.

It was a small, dingy, unventilated place that smelled of sweat and looked like a run-down gym you might find in a Hollywood movie. This was the kind of place that only the truly serious fighters would train—it was certainly no luxury health club. The fragrance, to me, was not sweat; it was success. I was sold on it immediately and joined the same day.

My first sparring match was to determine my level of expertise. I sized up my competition and snickered quietly to myself with arrogance. He was a smaller Japanese fighter who I knew I could easily defeat. I was bigger and clearly stronger. He would also underestimate me as a beginner for little did he know I'd been practicing.

The sparring match was over quickly. Lesson one; don't underestimate smaller guys and don't ever assume you know what you're doing. In short, I got my ass kicked.

In fact, everyone I fought that day seemed better than the one before. Clearly, I had come to the right place. Equally clearly, I was in need of some serious training. It was a humbling experience; every single day I worked out with these fighters. Lesson two; size and strength don't always give you an advantage; it's often your expertise and skill in a system of fighting.

With an almost Biblical resolve, I trained for thirty straight days and dreamed about it for thirty straight nights. I trained harder than I ever thought possible. I wanted so badly to test what I had learned, but the fear of humiliation in front of my teacher, and what seemed to be the whole world, held me back. After all, just because I thought I was ready didn't make it so. As with any arena of intense focus, at that point in my life it seemed that the entire world established the value of a human being on his martial arts prowess. I didn't care about a college education, money, a social life or even that I was thousands of miles away from home and family in a land where people barely understood what I was saying. I spoke with my body and slept when I felt I had earned it.

Finally, after one particularly hard day of training, I approached my coach, Kawaguchi Kenji. Nervously, I asked him when he thought I would be ready. I wanted his opinion as to when he felt I was ready to fight—ready to win. I was shocked when he said he'd sign me up for the next big event which was going to be held at the world famous Super Tiger Gym.

It also came as a shock that he already seemed to have confidence in my fighting abilities. His attitude actually helped spur on my self-confidence.

The Super Tiger Gym was an exciting venue and certainly very significant in the world of Shooto. Sayama Satoru, a famous Japanese pro-wrestler who went by the name of Tiger Mask, owned it. He also just happened to be the man who established Shooto. Shooto, a mixed martial arts organization is the result of Sayama's desire to evolve his professional wrestling and catch wrestling styles into an effective fighting system. It originated in 1985, but didn't go pro until 1989. Shooto hosted the original Vale Tudo Japan event in 1994.

Shooto utilizes striking—based on karate and muay thai, the wrestling and judo takedowns, and the submissions from catch wrestling and judo. Sayama's style of training yielded well-rounded mixed martial arts fighters.

It's important to appreciate the significance of fighting in the Super Tiger Gym. This was the birthplace of a world-recognized sport—not a wanna-be emulation, but where it actually began. I had come so far and risked so much to be in this mecca of my profession.

Sayama's infamous gym was well known for its brutal training methods and aggressive style. It was also known for pumping out great champions and that's exactly what I planned to be—a great champion.

Sayama's brutal training methods were evident in a video hosted online as he repeatedly hit the student he was training in the face. A link to this video may be found on the Facebook page for this book and the translation is as follows:

Sayama: Kick the mitts.

Student kicks…

Sayama: Kick the mitts stronger; as hard as you can.

Student: Okay.

Sayama: If I tell you to kick as hard as you can, you have to do it. Do you understand?

Student: Yes, I understand.

Sayama: Are you messing with me?

Student: No…

Sayama: I said kick as hard as you can! Was that the hardest you can kick?

Student: Yes

Sayama: That was the hardest you can kick?

Student: Student doesn't reply; Silence…

Sayama: Are you messing with me?

Student: No…

Sayama Kick as hard as you can! (Hits student)

Student kicks… (Gets hit)

Sayama: Do it! I'll kill you!

Student kicks… (Gets hit)

Sayama: Kick as hard as you can! (Hits student)

Student kicks… (Gets hit)

Sayama repeats himself: Kick as hard as you can! Again!

Sayama: I want you guys to do this for each other. All I'm doing is helping you. Do this for each other. Do it for yourself. Do you understand?

Students: Yes, we understand.

I never got to train directly under Tiger Mask, but my coach, Kawaguchi-san, was one of his disciples and he was very good at what he did. He also happened to be the former Shooto Light Heavyweight Champion, so I was clearly in good hands and I knew that this placed yet another advantage in my repertoire. There were, after all, so many disadvantages already in my path.

The plan was that I would be fighting three different fights, on three different days, and in three different events. They would take place over a span of three months and would all be held at the Super Tiger Gym. Was I ready? You bet I was!

When the day of the first fight dawned, my stomach was tighter than a wound clock. There was simply so much at stake. In one sense, this day represented a reckoning; it would tell me, as well as the world, whether my decision to choose martial arts as a profession, and whether my moving to Japan, was all worth it. I wouldn't have to face it alone, however.

My father had timed a visit to be there with me. He arrived at the same airport I had, in Narita. That was where I'd had my encounter with the custom's officers.

The following day, my dad went with me to the Shooting Gym Yokohama to watch me train. I was so excited he was there and couldn't wait to show him what I had learned. I introduced him to my coaches and training partners, but while the language barrier precluded any long discussions, the civilities were observed.

Just like when I was a kid, my dad stood on the sidelines as I sparred and shouted instructions. Although his knowledge of MMA was limited, he gave me the benefit of everything he knew. It was so good to have him by my side again and it made me feel less alone. He had just arrived in Japan; this made me want to win for him even more. I was proud and wanted him to realize I truly had a future.

This brought about a conversation regarding college. Upon my return to Japan in January I was supposed to have attended classes locally at the Friend's World Program's Japanese Center. It had been the plan to complete my homework assignments weekly and hand them in, but between work and training, I simply couldn't find the time to commit to one more thing. That's when my dad and I had a long conversation about what I hoped to accomplish in the future. That's when I decided to drop out of college and pursue a career as a mixed martial artist full time. Since my parents were both teachers, this didn't make them particularly happy. Nevertheless, Dad overcame his disappointment and supported me in my decision.

Before Dad left I introduced him to David and Gloria. My dad went to great length to thank them for all they'd done for me.

We also took a trip to Kyoto and spent some time seeing the country. Kyoto is one of Asia's oldest and most famous metropolises, well known for it's beautiful temples and parks.

My dad's visit was a shining example of the dedication he showed to me right from my birth. I was nervous and wanted to get the fight started quickly. Having my father there in some ways made me even more nervous. I knew he believed in me. I wanted to live up to his expectations… *My* expectations…

I recall doubting myself over and over again as I stood there mentally preparing for the battle to come. *Was I really ready for this or was I about to have my lunch fed to me?* After all, it hadn't been all that long since the day I began my training and got my ass kicked by a bunch of martial artists smaller and weaker than me. I stand 5'5" and am very strong; but as I had learned, that isn't always enough. My prayers were answered when I won the first match in my amateur debut with an arm bar in the first round.

Shortly after that I was asked by Kawaguchi-san whether I would like to attend Enson Inoue's seminar. He didn't have to ask twice. Inoue is a mixed martial artist of Japanese American descent and a former Shooto Heavyweight Champion. His famous win over former UFC Heavyweight Champion Randy Couture in 1998 would be later featured in the documentary *Rites of Passage*. He also made an appearance in *Redbelt*, a martial arts movie.

It would be my first meeting with Enson, but at the seminar I didn't get a chance to speak with him directly. After the seminar I found out much more about him by renting Shooto videos at a local store near the gym.

Encouraged by my burgeoning success, my second fight was against a Japanese guy with dreadlocks. I won this fight by decision after a hard-fought battle for position and trading leg locks. It wasn't an easy match, but whenever you come out the victor, it's always a good match.

It was after this second match that I injured my knee. It happened in a leg lock; a common injury in Japanese gyms but relatively uncommon the in the U.S. at the time, hence I had to learn the hard way. You will see fighters wrapping their knees heavily prior to training due to the high rate of injury. I had originally hurt my knee by being heel-hooked during my training. A heel hook is a dangerous leg lock with a high rate of injury, especially to the ligaments.

Mine happened in training one day. I was working from the bottom position when my sparring partner sat back from within my guard and attempted a leg lock. I rolled to try and escape and my opponent rolled with it. I was stuck and couldn't get out. We both heard the telltale *pop* when I tried to escape; my ligaments had torn. Others heard the sound as well and they rushed to my side and urged me to ice the injury immediately.

I couldn't afford health insurance at the time and couldn't pay for the x-rays the hospital wanted. The doctor recommended I let the injury heal and I complied, but only until the fight. I simply sucked it up and fought it.

I began to prepare for my third fight against the future Shooto Welterweight Champion and Pride Lightweight Champion, Gomi Takanori. He was the last and only Pride Lightweight Champion; once considered the best pound-for-pound fighter in the world.

This was the first time we fought. Going into the fight my mind was filled with doubt; hoping my knee would hold up.

I overestimated my health, though, and the fight proved it.

I re-injured my knee during that day and lost it, 8-0. My knee wasn't the only thing injured—my pride hurt the worst.

In amateur Shooto, points are earned for effective strikes, takedowns, and improving one's position. Despite my loss, due to my strong showing and heart in that match, I ended up being invited to the All-Japan Amateur Shooto Tournament. Back then you needed to place in the top three in the All-Japan Tournament to earn the right to turn pro, which of course was my ultimate goal. This invitation gave me yet another boost to my confidence.

In preparation for the tournament, a three-day weekend *Gashiku* was held for those of us who trained at the same gym. A *Gashiku* typically refers to an intensive training period that can last for several days. During that time you train, eat and sleep together. Most gyms hold these training sessions in the summertime as well as in the winter.

This training really pushed me mentally and physically. Prior to this, I had trained hard, but did not have cardiovascular conditioning. We added a long run at the beginning and end of our training. I remember feeling my side burn—the sort you get in your ribcage when you're not in shape. It hurt badly.

Even so, in August of 1998, just five short months after officially joining Shooting Gym Yokohama, I placed in the tournament top three. The time had come for me to turn pro.

There was just one major problem. My coach didn't think I was ready yet, and in hindsight, he was probably right. Nevertheless I was determined, young and feeling more self-assured than I had in my life. When you're a mixed martial artist, belief in yourself is almost as important as the training. When one or the other is lacking, you risk serious injury and humiliation.

I had an opportunity to speak with Enson before the All-Japan Tournament commenced. It was an all-day event, and

I used that opportunity to pick his brain. I'm not sure he understood the significance of our talk, but I hung on every word and watched every reaction he had. I tried to absorb the essence of the sport from him by osmosis.

I learned that he was born in Hawaii but was of Japanese descent and was, indeed, the current Shooto Heavyweight Champion of the world. We had great chemistry almost immediately. I explained to him that I was thinking about moving back to America to turn pro and he suggested that if I did, I should seek out and train with the reigning UFC Middleweight Champion, Frank Shamrock, the brother of world-renowned Ken Shamrock. Ken needs absolutely no introduction to MMA fans.

Enson went on to explain how good Frank Shamrock really was as a fighter and that he, Enson, had just lost to Frank in the prestigious Vale Tudo Japan event held by Shooto. Upon hearing all that, I was more excited and motivated than ever to turn pro as soon as possible.

If it was possible, I became even more focused than I had been before. I started a vigorous training schedule that included seven days a week. It was tough living in filth and struggling for every dollar, or should I say Yen, but I think it also helped build my character. In some ways, the grittier my living circumstances became, the harder I worked to overcome them and reach toward my fighting potential. I had the confidence to fight on a professional level. Moreover, I knew I could win. That combination meant I could earn more money while realizing one of my lifelong dreams. Those are the things that kept me going when my body was tired and my stomach hungry.

Constantly on the lookout for any reading material about martial arts, one day I came across a magazine with Frank Shamrock on the cover. I got even more excited to note that it listed his website. It seemed he was preparing to develop a fight team. He was testing candidates back in the States.

That was all I needed to read. I sent him an email immediately and hoped I might get a response someday. Someday came the very next day in the form of an email response. I held my breath and paused for a second in anticipation as I opened the email. Amazingly, Shamrock simply wrote me back and immediately invited me to the testing. I couldn't believe he got back to me so quickly, and the response was absolutely magical. I read it three times in excited disbelief. *Had Frank Shamrock really invited me to test before him?* You bet he had. It was settled. I was ready to go. I would travel back to the U.S. and test for Frank Shamrock's team. In fact I would do better than that. I would test and I would succeed – at least that was the goal. Nothing would stand in my way!

Chapter Ten

American Training

It was finally September of 1998 and I was moving back the U.S., to San Jose. Frank Shamrock, himself, met me at the airport.

I remember watching him walk toward me. I was overwhelmed by his size; he was huge! Not necessarily in height but he was *very* muscular. I was not a small man, but he looked strong enough to break my hand when he shook it. When we shook hands, it was firm but not competitive. In fact, if anything, it was welcoming.

Frank was on his way to a radio interview nearby and offered to pick me up. I was very flattered by his informality; it was as if we were already good friends and yet we had only just met.

Frank climbed into his sporty convertible with an air of nonchalance and success. It was abundantly clear that he had no need to work a supplemental 9 to 5 job. He made his living doing what he loved; indeed, the sport I loved. I saw myself in his shoes, and not too far in the future.

I went along on that interview and afterwards he dropped me off at my hotel. As I slowly walked up to my room I couldn't help but wonder about the next day; the day when I would show Frank Shamrock what I was made of. *But what if I don't make it? What if the testing is harder than I anticipated?* Doubts raced through my mind like a runaway freight train and I tried to remember the way Frank carried himself—like a winner. I wouldn't get where he was by doubting myself. I had to stop thinking like that. I *knew* I was good enough to be there and I *knew* I was good enough to excel.

I ended up lying awake for hours that night. When I finally did close my eyes to sleep, it seemed like only minutes before the alarm shrilled into the dim light of the morning. I awoke and rolled from the bed with attitude. I was a champion and I knew it. It was time the world knew it, too.

I found my way to Frank's gym, the American Kickboxing Academy (AKA), which was very well known in the States. Javier Mendez, a former world kickboxing champion, owned it. I didn't know a great deal about Javier at the time, but then I really didn't need to. Frank Shamrock trained there and that was all the qualifications I needed.

Frank had grown up in a boys' home for troubled youth. Bob Shamrock and his wife, Dee Dee, in Susanville, California, owned it. Here Frank met Ken, who had originally come to Bob's home under the supervision of a parole officer at the age of 13 with a history of violence, rage and an estrangement from his family. By the time Ken was in high school, he could already bench press 360 pounds. Frank was no softie, himself, and he grew even tougher as a protégé, and later the adopted son, of Bob Shamrock, as had Ken. Bob's strategy was to give the tough guys enough work and training to keep them out of trouble.

Ken developed a career in mixed martial arts, in Pancrase, a rival of Shooto in Japan and then fought in the UFC from 1993 to 1996. Frank learned MMA from Ken as his first teacher and owner of the gym, the Lion's Den. Eventually the two had a falling out and Frank left the Den to learn other techniques.

Until this time, MMA had been dominated by Brazilian jiu-jitsu initially and later by wrestlers. It was now the time to become a truly well-rounded athlete and Frank was on the scene. He showed up at Javier Mendez's American Kickboxing Academy one day and started learning to kickbox. He trained at San Jose State University and worked out with some of their top wrestlers.

Frank also had a good friend and pro kickboxer, Maurice Smith. They had been good friends and training partners since their days at the Lion's Den. Frank later started his own MMA team (Team USA) at American Kickboxing Academy (AKA). Today, AKA is one of the top five gyms in America and currently has several fighters fighting in the UFC including the two-time UFC Heavyweight Champion, Cain Velasquez.

Frank Shamrock ran his program out of the Kickboxing Academy and helped them start their mixed martial arts program.

Bright and early the next morning I arrived with anxiety, fear and a determination to have a successful test. I discovered that very few people ever actually passed the test and that almost nobody ever did it on their first attempt. *Great*, I grimly reflected. *This is all my nerves need to hear!* I learned that not only would most candidates end up bruised and battered, but it wasn't rare to get seriously injured. This was stern stuff and aspiring fighters had to be at the top of their game. This was a do-or-die situation for me; I made completely sure I was ready. Sure, I was a little frightened, that was only normal, but it's what a champion does with that fear that will separate him from the rest.

I converted my fear into a power. I envisioned a transparent dome of invincibility and energy, drawing it mentally down to encase my body. I used it to feed strength to my legs, speed to my arms and power to my takedowns.

The test was intense. It involved hundreds up push-ups, sit-ups, squats, leg lifts, and too many exercises to list. The intent was to test my "fight or flight" mentality.

The opponents lined up to give me a beating, but I took it well. They were all bigger and fresher than I felt; not exhausted from push-ups and squats like I was, but I ignored the pain and continued fighting. My legs were burning and my arms were limp, but my spirit and resolve was as strong as ever. I was going to do this and I was going to succeed. I held the boundaries of my invisible dome intact and nothing but positive intensity could penetrate my thoughts.

It had its rewards. I made the team! There is nothing to compare with the exhilaration that gave me. Not only was I part of a world-class fighting machine, but also I had passed on my first attempt and the damage was minimal, or so I hoped. Nothing could have foretold the utter agony I suffered for the next seven days. My determination and resolve survived, though, and I could tell that even the famous Frank Shamrock, not to mention everyone else there in the gym that morning, was impressed by my fighting skills and sheer heart. My pain was diminished with the exuberance of success and pride.

I needed a job. My plan was to stay in the States while I trained. For a while I worked in construction and at Starbucks. For the foreseeable future my life became a brutal cycle of early rising to dig pipe trenches, brew pungent coffee and then cut to the gym to beat my body into excellence.

The true value of this period of time was that I learned I *hated* construction. I had never worked hard labor before and I found this work hot and the sun unforgiving. My clothes were layered with grime within 20 minutes of starting and I learned how much I hated being dirty. Shovel after shovel, I could feel the fatigue from training the day before.

My housing for the time being consisted of sleeping on a teammate's sofa, and that got old really quickly. It was time to head back to Japan and train from there; so that's exactly what I did. It was extremely tiring and I felt drained all the time, but that's where the mental discipline kicks in for a martial artist. When work ended, the training began. I almost forgot what it felt like to rest.

Chapter Eleven

Gone from California…

The teammate who put me up was named Charles. He had a nice apartment, but the neighborhood was decidedly in trouble. It was in a predominately Hispanic part of San Jose. One day as I was getting ready to leave the house, his brother, Giorgio, warned me the purple sweatpants I had donned wouldn't be a good idea in their neighborhood. It seemed this was a gang color and that was enough to make me change immediately. I'd forgotten what it was to be concerned about such things. Street gangs were not a problem I needed to think about in Japan.

Up to this point I hadn't experienced any problems with the cyst in my brain. I tried not to think about it and instead focused on the fact that I hated the drudgery of my prison-like hard labor and I would rather return to relative poverty in Japan and train full time than to remain in San Jose. As a matured fighter today I would have told myself to suck it up, but at the time it was all the excuse I needed to book a flight westward.

I also simply missed Japan, and my sport was still illegal in most of the U.S. There was more money to be made in Japan and I knew that's where I belonged. What I didn't know, however, was that in Japan, expats and highly paid foreigners are usually found and hired outside of Japan. Living locally and speaking Japanese worked against you in this sense. In retrospect, it would have been professionally easier and far more lucrative to get a fighting contract in Japan while living elsewhere.

Thus, in January of 1999 I was on my way back to Japan for more training. I was now technically fighting under Frank Shamrock and just the thought of that gave me new incentive. A female associate of his, Kobayashi Hidemi, acted as my manager in his absence and managed me in Japan. Kobayashi-san and I eventually became very good friends; she came to be a big sister to me while I was in Japan. We are still very close to this day.

When it came to Shooto, I was fighting freelance—not under the name of an official gym. Combine that with the fact that I was managed, and by a woman, yet, and it's apparent I was breaking ground in every sense. I met Kobayashi-san that same month through Frank who was in Japan briefly to corner one of my teammates, Charles, from America in a Shooto event.

Kobayashi-san withstood significant criticism in Japan for the fact that she was a woman working in the fight business. Ironically, one man, who shall remain nameless, called her for advice in making connections. Two years later, though, her contribution and wisdom were conveniently overlooked when he achieved a level of success.

This was an example of another aspect of the Japanese culture I was not accustomed to. Women are seldom praised or treated equally, as compared to their male counterparts. I know it still happens in America, but Japan takes female oppression to a whole new, almost extreme level. Even today, it's not uncommon for a female graduate of a prestigious school, regardless of her education, to serve tea to all her colleagues in a predominately male work environment.

I re-established the same dirty residence I had maintained before at the *gaijin house* in Ishikawacho, Yokohama; this time, on the third floor. If anything, it was even dirtier than the second floor I lived on a year earlier.

It seemed people living on the third floor were more into partying than working full time. It was noisy, loud and where I'd at least shared a window the year before, now I lacked one entirely. This meant the complete absence of ventilation and that made the room smell horrible.

Little by little, I was gaining more confidence in my ability to speak Japanese. When I had a little extra money, I escaped my filthy confines and walked to a nearby *sento* where I could bathe properly; I just needed to feel clean. A *sento* is a traditional Japanese bathhouse. It's similar to a city-water version of a mineral hot spring.

While tattoos are usually banned from these types of establishments this one allowed it, perhaps because many of their clients were *Yakuza*, or Japanese mafia. It cost about 400 yen ($4.00) each time so I couldn't go often.

When you enter, you purchase a ticket from a vending machine by the front door. You buy according to whether you want to just bathe, or to include the sauna. This machine was, of course, in Japanese only, which was another example of why learning the language was so critical to my living there.

After receiving a locker key at the front desk, you enter the changing room. There are small lockers for your belongings.

Instead of taking a shower, at a *sento*, you have many small, knee-height faucets. You choose a stool from a stack near the entrance to the shower room and sit before the faucets, washing yourself with soap. Only after washing thoroughly are you allowed to get into the various bathtubs.

There were several types: Chinese herbal, Jacuzzi, foot massage, and electric bath. The electric is just as it sounds like. It was a bathtub filled with water. It had an electric current that travels through it.

Afterwards, I always felt refreshed and certainly improved over the bathing available on the *gaijin house* third floor.

Chapter Twelve

The Business of Fighting

While fighting freelance technically gave me the freedom to do so, I didn't understand at the time that jumping back and forth from America to Japan was not working in my favor. I was still young and very naive. I also soon discovered that this lack of representation by a gym was highly frowned upon by the Japanese. They are deeply rooted in tradition and new concepts, including freelancing, were not readily accepted in those days, although this has changed recently. The Japanese already were very traditional and had difficulty anticipating upcoming changes.

I suppose it was just my thoroughly American independence that had not changed simply because of where I was living. That zero-tolerance for anything or anyone who didn't fall in line with tradition became something I eventually learned to despise about Japan. Regardless, I had to make a living, so my options were very limited.

At the time, I was working as a bus boy at a French restaurant in Roppongi, an eclectic Minato ward of Tokyo that contained some very plush spots. Although I didn't realize it at the time, Roppongi was renowned for its clubbing and red light district. The sleaziness was around me all the time and I wasn't even aware of it.

When business grew slow at the restaurant, I was let go and suddenly found myself unemployed. The owner was French. He was all business and this set the tone from the beginning; when the restaurant opened. One thing was obvious; he didn't care about his staff and could be extremely condescending. I was literally fired on the spot and not even permitted to finish out the day's work. I tried not to read French stereotypes into this fact, but it would be the experience of being fired on the spot that formed my opinion about working for others. I knew, that given the opportunity, I would never again allow a single company complete control over my livelihood and I finally understood why my grandfather preferred to work for himself.

But as they say, every cloud has a silver lining and mine was that this freed me to train full time. However, without a job I didn't have enough money for food or even the next month's rent.

Fortunately, the very next day Frank Shamrock informed me that I was booked in an eight-man tournament in Waikiki, Hawaii, appropriately called the "Super Brawl." Super Brawl Icon Sport is a mixed martial arts organization based in Honolulu. The organization has one of the longest-running promotions, dating back to 1995. The promotion has recently been renamed as Icon Sport, omitting the "Super Brawl" prefix.

Considering what faced me in the upcoming tournament, food and shelter might become the least of my worries. I was learning quickly that when reality crashes head-on with your dreams, sometimes those dreams have to take a back seat. I was determined to not let that happen. I didn't know how yet, but somehow I was going to continue my training and still eat right up until my pro-debut as a fighting warrior.

~

It was during this preparation that I got knocked out.

~

I began to prepare for the fight. It was during this preparation that while sparring hard at the gym, I got knocked out.

I wobbled toward home, alone, dazed and dizzy from being knocked unconscious. I knew in my gut that getting hit like that so close to a fight made it a bad idea to compete, but at that point I had no choice because rent would be due soon and I had no other means of making money at the time. I realized that at some point in my life I would need to cut loose from my supporting part-time jobs and become a dedicated fighter.

Not only was I unemployed with no money for food or rent, but I could not afford medical care. I didn't even have a valid working visa, much less health insurance.

By the time I finally got home, I realized I had a concussion. That night I set my alarm to wake myself every few hours to make sure I was okay. I remember feeling very lonely in my time of need. It certainly wasn't what I wanted, but there was no other choice. There was no one close to me I could ask for help; I was truly on my own.

So, it happened that in February 1999, I made my pro debut in Waikiki, Hawaii. Some of my friends from the *gaijin house* shared in the excitement of my pro debut. One of them, a guy named Jon, had worked as a hair stylist in the U.K. and offered to bleach my hair. So there I was, sitting in the communal living area with plastic wrap wound around my head, waiting for the chemicals to kick in. Once it was all finished, my hair was blond. I thought bleaching would make a statement—to encourage fans to remember me, not only for my fighting style, but also for being different than all the rest. Around the *gaijin house* this crazy hairdo earned me the nickname "Guinness" after the Irish beer.

* * * * *

I was one of eight fighters selected to compete in this tournament. On the opposite bracket was a fellow Shooto fighter, Oishi Masahiro, who had far more experience than I. The Japanese community had very high hopes for him and he had been chosen by Shooto to represent them in the tournament.

Losing and failure was not an option for me. The weight of the world was on his shoulders and I hoped his mental strength wasn't as great as his physical ability. To make the 150-lb weight limit for my fight I needed to diet hard, which always made me a little weaker.

No job meant having no money for food, so I turned to a diet of rice and pasta. As what little money I had left began to run out, I ate yogurt for breakfast and dinner. At this time, I was still learning about nutrition and how it played a major role. My stomach growled constantly and it was hard to maintain a hard workout schedule and not feel run down.

I remember waking up the morning just before I headed to the airport. I sat up on my futon, looked around at my dismal living conditions and thought to myself, *I have to win. I don't want to live like this anymore.*

When I arrived that afternoon at the Narita International Airport for my flight to Hawaii, I was informed, matter-of-factly, that the airplane's main engine had failed. This was devastating news and a distraction I didn't need. I simply had to get to Hawaii in time to rest before my fights and anything that threatened the routine could be potentially devastating for me. A failed engine wasn't in my plans, but winning was.

I ended up staying at a hotel not too far from the airport while my new flight was being organized. This meant that instead of getting a good night's rest, I would be forced to fight tired the next day; never a good thing. But I was getting pretty good at playing the cards I had been dealt, and this was no different.

I was traveling with a Japanese reporter, Takashima Manabu, who was covering the event for the Japanese media. Even he realized how devastating this turn of events was for me. I finally arrived in Hawaii at 5:30 on the morning of the event, and salvaged a couple of hours' sleep before meeting with Frank Shamrock to prepare. Once you have turned pro, promotions provide accommodations and the bigger organizations also provide a food allowance.

Lucky for me, the fight was that evening. I told him what had happened at the airport and I could see the concern in his eyes.

Nevertheless, he assured me, "You can do this, Ryan," and I believed him. I *could* do this, sleep or no sleep. This was my day to prove something to myself and to the world. It was my opportunity to show that I truly was a champion and nothing would deter me from that goal.

As the tournament began, the Japanese fighter, Oishi Masahiro, for whom the Japanese had held such high hopes, was knocked out in the first round.

I was pitted against Erik Rysher in the first round. To say I was nervous would be an understatement. Between the lack of sleep, the travel and the fact that my very survival hung in the balance, I felt the tension with every ounce of my being. It was my first fight as a professional in a place I'd never been to before and I told myself I was here to fight. I focused enough to redirect the anxiety into the reason I had come.

Once my opponent and I made eye contact and touched gloves, the fight was on. I immediately shot in with a double leg takedown and secured top position. With that takedown, I was able to set the pace of the fight and began to relax. This was where I felt most comfortable, on the ground. I quickly passed my opponent's guard and finished the fight with an arm bar from the mount position at the one-minute seventeen-second mark of the fight.

The nerves were gone and now I was in the zone, ready to attack fast and hard. My second fight was against Matt Hamilton and it took even less time. I attacked my opponent violently and scored first with a powerful knee to his midsection just before I got the takedown. I mounted him and rained down punches to get him to expose an arm. He eventually did just that, so I spun to the side in an attempt to secure an arm bar, but the referee briefly got in the way. I hesitated. Frank yelled, "It's not over yet. You have to finish it!" from my corner. This got my attention and I quickly secured the arm bar to end the fight. My opponent was upset about the referee's unintentional interference, but it was too late. I had earned my position in the finals.

Between fights I calculated how much money I had won so far; I still needed to pay rent when I got back home to Japan. For the next few months this would be my guiding priority. Frank Shamrock came up to me before my final fight and I could tell he was impressed by my first two bouts. He also seemed a little surprised—in an excited and supportive way. I knew he believed in me, although it was encouraging to be accomplishing so much this quickly. It seemed all my hard work and dedication were finally worth it—and I would have money to prove it.

"I'm right here with you," Shamrock said, intensity in his eyes. It echoed my thoughts. I had trained hard for this. Losing now was not an option. Frank refused to let me see the fight that would determine my third opponent. It was too brutal.

He came in the package of the boxer, Cheyenne Padeken; the same fighter who had knocked out the Japanese fighter, Oishi Masahiro, in the first round of the tournament.

There I was, on one of the world's most beautiful islands; an American fighting on American soil, an accomplishment I could only achieve by living in Japan. I had made it to the finals and I didn't come for second place.

It was time to fight and my plan was simple. I was more of a grappler than a striker, so I took the fight to the ground almost immediately, this time with a body-lock. I clinched his lower back and squeezed hard, forcing his back to give way and allowing me to throw him to the mat. My goal was to tie him up to keep him from throwing damaging punches. I quickly secured his arm with an arm bar and later learned his corner man had thrown in the towel to forfeit the match, but apparently the referee never saw it and unlike in my first two fights, this opponent was able to fight himself free.

I rose to my feet breathing heavily because I had put all my strength into the arm bar. I remember thinking to myself, *damn, he got out! I'm tired!*

The fight continued and I got another takedown using a body-lock, only this time I mounted him and threw a barrage of hard punches to his face, forcing him to turn his back. Once he did that, I forced him into submission with a rear chokehold, holding… holding… and won the tournament! I felt a rush of the remaining adrenalin at the success of my strategy. I had fought hard and come out unscathed.

I was ecstatic! There could be no more glorious way to earn my living. After winning three fights and becoming the Lightweight Tournament Champion I had made $1,500. I was young and had tasted success. This meant that for even a very short time, I could forget about the conditions I had to endure in Japan.

Chapter Thirteen

Lightweight Champion

There was nothing that could compare to the exhilaration I felt after my big win in Hawaii. I had gone with a wish and come back with my dream. Nothing, however, is ever that simple. My ability to live in Japan was now threatened.

I had been traveling in and out of Japan on a tourist visa ever since dropping out of college. Therefore, within three months of becoming the 1999 Super Brawl Lightweight Tournament Champion and returning to Japan, my 90-day tourist visa was about to expire. Having come in and out so many times, I risked being permanently deported—which obviously would impair any type of future in the country.

Japanese immigration is very vigilant regarding tourist visas. Most tourists enter with a return ticket to their own country already in hand. If you don't have this, it will raise a red flag with the Japanese officials. In my case, my return ticket was just around the corner. If I chose not to use it, I would have to either stay in Japan under the radar illegally or return to the US. The penalty for overstaying my 90-day tourist visa would be deportation and denial to re-enter Japan for five years. Obviously this would be out of the question for me.

Thus, the difficulty in getting my visa renewed found me returning to Grand Rapids in April of 1999. I lived at home to save as much money as I possibly could. I began teaching MMA at the Kung Fu school where I had begun training. At the same time, I also began working as a waiter at a local Italian restaurant, Pietros. These combined positions earned me only about $1,000 per month. My goal was simple; to be able to finance a return to San Jose where I could rejoin Frank's fight team.

My plan took hold a few months later when I found myself back in San Jose and Frank was able to again book me in Super Brawl, the same Hawaiian event as before. To prepare, I spent a month, training three times a day, six days a week at AKA in San Jose.

Every morning we would wake up and do cardio at 24 Hour Fitness. Our cardio routines consisted of 30 minutes of interval training and sprints, ensuring that we could keep an intense pace while working out at 85% of our max heart rate.

In the afternoon we made the 30-minute drive down to AKA to get in some ring time. Each of us was required to spar three, 5-minute rounds against a fresh opponent who would technically be at our level. We got pretty banged up in sparring, but this prepared us for what we would have to endure in the ring.

We spent hours every evening meticulously working on our technique. From working on setting up our takedowns with strikes (punches and kicks) against the pressure of specially-designed resistance bands, to defending ourselves and fighting back to a standing position from various bottom positions; we worked on every aspect of the game.

Nights found me sleeping on Charles' sofa once again. It was not a life of luxury but I was grateful for his generosity and it allowed me to fight. That's all that mattered.

Back in Honolulu, Hawaii for Super Brawl; this time I fought against Brennan Kamaka. He fought out of the Jesus is Lord Gym, a name that I found very strange. It was formed by a group of born-again Christians who found Christ as troubled youths. I never understood the concept of punching each other in the face as worshipful. Even though it's a competition, it just seemed fundamentally wrong.

I immediately clinched Brennan in the corner and fought hard for the takedown. As his lower back was giving out, he grabbed the ropes illegally to avoid being taken down. This forced me to end up on bottom in the guard position. I quickly attacked and spun for an arm bar from guard position. His elbow popped as I applied the arm bar and swept him over onto his back.

I won the fight in Super Brawl in the first round by submission and the purse was $500. I was thrilled with my growing success, but just wasn't happy living in America. I wanted to return to Japan as quickly as I could. I was homesick for a land that wasn't my own, and the feeling was terrible.

* * * * *

I wanted to be the full package. I'd long been fascinated by muay thai, a combat martial art sport known as "the art of eight limbs" due to its eight points of contact by combined use of feet, shins, knees, elbows and fists.

Thus, before returning to Japan, in November of 1999, I travelled to Thailand to finally train muay thai and do it in the country where it all began.

Thailand is an amazing country, beautiful to look at but hellish in its climate. It was hot and humid all year around, quite different from what I was accustomed to.

I chose to go to the island of Koh Samui, located in the south of Thailand and home to some of the world's most beautiful beaches. I hoped that at least those beaches would be a welcome relief from the staggering humidity. The trip was both for training and vacation purposes.

I trained at Lamai Muay Thai Camp. Gyms in Thailand differ from what I'd been used to in the U.S. and Japan in that they are outdoors. It consisted of a ring and several heavy bags, not to mention a full compliment of really tough fighters.

In the West we fight martial arts by choice. We have a genuine interest in it so we set out to learn more. In stark contrast, though, despite being Thailand's national sport, muay thai is, for many, a way out of poverty. Affluent Thais look down on the sport but those less fortunate see it as a way to better their lives. It isn't uncommon for gyms to take in troubled youth, enroll them in school and train them in muay thai, so it was a great vehicle for impoverished and troubled kids. Boys, as young as ten, would turn pro and fight to earn a living. It's a brutal culture and was very different from anything I was accustomed to.

Comparing their lifestyle to how I had grown up, and watching young kids go through so much, really made me cherish what I had. By comparison, even as poor as I was right now, the simple freedom of fighting as a choice rather than necessity to escape from deep poverty or abuse made me feel quite fortunate.

* * * * *

After returning to Grand Rapids from Thailand, it was time to do something I vowed I never would. I decided to teach English. I had avoided it like the plague because of a need to learn the Japanese language. This meant to *really* learn it well, and not just be content speaking a broken version of it to get by.

I decided to get licensed to become an English Language (ESL) teacher. It was the only option I had if I wanted to get a proper "working visa" and return to Japan. As always, I did what was needed to get the job done.

I attended Transworld Schools in San Francisco and graduated late 1999.

The following January I returned to Japan and when I arrived, I immediately booked a room at the same gaijin house in Yokohama City. Once again I was starting out and my choices were very limited. At least there I knew what to expect.

However, to my delight, this would soon change. Now that I was a certified ESL teacher, I was able to get a job at Gaba One to One English School in Yokohama. This provided me with stable income while I trained and worked my way up the Shooto rankings. I worked full time, occasionally worked overtime, and trained full time. It was hard, but I was motivated to succeed.

Teaching English at Gaba was not something I wanted to do; it was not something I respected as a career long-term (for native English speakers) because it required no commitment to learning the Japanese language and truly living "the Japanese way". True immersion into the culture is impossible as an English teacher. That said, it paid much better than being a waiter. I made 250,000 yen or $2,500 per month at Gaba.

It wasn't long before I was able to rent my first apartment. This was easier said than done, however, as Japanese landlords often refuse to rent to foreigners. It's not looked upon as being racism, but simply a manner of conducting business. Conditional to moving in, you could expect to pay several things in advance. The first was one or two month's deposit. This will be refunded, minus cleaning fees, when you move out. You must also pay a month or two of what is known as "key money." This is gift money to the landlord to express gratitude for allowing you to live there. This is, incidentally, non-refundable. Next, you must pay the first month's rent and after that, you had to have a guarantor. This is a co-signer, of sorts, who agrees to take the responsibility for payment should you not be able to pay as promised.

Many Japanese are lucky enough to be able to have their parents co-sign for them, but this is usually not an option for foreigners. There are "guarantor companies" that will do it but this comes at a price—usually 1 month's rent.

So, before you can move in the front door, it's going to cost you four to six month's rent, up front. My first apartment was a 1DK; a 1 bedroom, dining area, and kitchen. The apartment building was old and was made of wood.

In Japan there are two kinds of apartments: mansions and apartments. Apartments are made of wood; mansions are made from concrete. Although similar in size, mansions are definitely made of better quality building materials.

My apartment was located in Katakuracho, a suburb of Yokohama City, and a short walk from a very busy street. It cost me 70,000 yen ($700 per month). When I moved in, it was absolutely filthy and clearly had not been lived in for a long time. There were cockroaches everywhere. The first thing I had to do was clean it from top to bottom—and then I started cleaning all over again.

It was a traditional Japanese apartment and had tatami mats as floors. These mats were traditionally made of rice straw and had a covering of woven soft rush. They have a long, traditional history and began in the homes of nobility. Today few homes in Japan have these but they are considered far more affordable.

Even though it wasn't what I would consider a nice apartment, it was a vast improvement from living at the *gaijin house*.

* * * * *

It took some time, but I finally started to get local fights in Shooto.

My first fight as a professional in Japan was versus Fujiwara Masato. Despite his tall stature, my plans going into this fight were to utilize my newly acquired muay thai skills and attack my opponent with vicious knees.

The fight went according to my game plan after I fought off my back and got back to the standing position after being taken down early on in the first round.

Immediately after standing up, I rushed my opponent with a barrage of punches; backing him up into the ropes. I latched onto his head with a thai plum position. The thai plum position is a traditional muay thai position in which you can control your opponent's posture by weighting down their torso to launch knees to their midsection and head.

I fired knee after knee. As each one landed, his body began to slump lower and lower. When he was slumped low enough for me to reach his head, I fired one last knee that caught him on the chin. He fell to the canvas immediately and it was evident he wasn't getting back up. I had won the fight in spectacular fashion and the crowd went wild.

Fujiwara was removed from the ring on a stretcher as I watched with mixed feelings. I made 70,000 yen or $700 for that fight.

One misconception people have about fighters is that we are violent and enjoy hurting people. As a professional, you take your trade very seriously. We don't get into the ring or cage to hurt our opponent. Sometimes it happens, but we are sportsmen first. Our sport is based on mutual respect among opponents. We do not hope they will be injured badly.

Desperate for revenge, I asked Shooto for another shot at fighting Gomi Takanori. He had beaten me when we were amateurs and I wanted a second chance. That finally happened in November of 2000. Gomi and I then fought as professionals. When the fight started, I was prepared to stand and trade punches and kicks with him. He, however, had other plans. After an exchange of punches, kicks, and knees, we clinched in the corner. From there, Gomi was able to take me down to the mat. I had blasted Gomi with a hard knee to his eye early in the fight and that got his attention. While I was on the mat I could tell that his eye was swelling up badly. In fact, it ended up breaking his orbital bone. In the third round Gomi took me down quickly and we continued to fight on the ground. The referee had to stop the fight so that the doctor could examine his eye. The fight should have been stopped for good right there, but it wasn't. You see with my being *gaijin*, it became obvious Shooto wanted Gomi to win the bout.

Although I like to think that I was slowly gaining fans and building a name for myself, I would be lying if I said I felt like I was always given a fair shot. Gomi went on to be an amazing champion and not to take anything from what he accomplished, but in this particular situation it was clear who the event promoters were hoping would win. This was in no way Gomi's fault, but an unfortunate reality that I would learn to accept and try to beat.

They allowed Gomi to continue fighting. He was a tough athlete and it showed. His wrestling was superior to mine and he seemed to absorb punishment very well. I struggled on the mat for most of the fight. Unfortunately for me, he was able to get another takedown and grind out a win by decision. This was my first loss as a pro, which made my record 6-1. I couldn't help but think that I should have wrestled more when my father tried to get me into the sport years earlier.

My father had always wanted me to wrestle. He stressed the importance of having wrestling as a skill-set because it would allow one to dictate where the fight takes place. I wish I had listened to him early on in my career. I remember him saying this the first time we ordered the UFC several years earlier.

Gomi was immediately taken to the hospital with his damaged eye and would eventually be out of competition for a year. Obviously the referee hadn't done him a favor by letting him continue the fight. I was paid 100,000 yen or $1,000 for the Gomi fight. One would have to wonder whether the purse was worth that to Gomi.

One thing I learned from the loss was that I needed to get better at grappling; avoid the takedown and fight better from the bottom position. Afterwards, I was invited to train in Tokyo at Wajutsu Keishukai. Wajutsu Keishukai had many top ranked fighters: Uno Kaoru, Toida Katsuya, Takase Daiju, and Okami Yushin to name a few.

My heroic attempt to defeat Gomi actually had an upside, though. It was shortly after that in December of 2000 when I got the offer from the UFC. Despite coming off a loss, it seemed that even the officials at the UFC believed I had actually won the fight! This happened while I was home in Grand Rapids for the Christmas holiday. I couldn't have asked for a better Christmas present.

Chapter Fourteen

The UFC

In January of 2001 I signed with the UFC to schedule a fight with Jens Pulver for the first ever Lightweight Championship of the world. The UFC, or Ultimate Fighting Championship is the host of worldwide mixed martial arts events, in fact they are the largest.

The 155 lb. weight class; my weight class, was now officially being recognized outside of Japan. The fight was scheduled to take place at UFC 30: "Battle on the Boardwalk" at the Trump Taj Mahal in Atlantic City, New Jersey. The stakes were high and I was well prepared.

Everything went as predicted until the UFC discovered the cyst in my head from a CT scan. All fighters must undergo medical exams, including CT scans, in order to be licensed by the athletic commission of the state where the event is being held. I have no clue how the public found out about the cyst and to this day it's still a mystery. Someone must have leaked the information before I was even told, because I found out the way everyone else did—on the Internet. My mind raced and I wanted answers. My dream of fighting in the UFC was in serious jeopardy. I would have made $3,000 for the fight versus Jens Pulver.

* * * * *

In those years, the sport of MMA was still fighting for legitimacy in the U.S. and the UFC was heading the battle with a new management company, Zuffa.

Since the biggest fights were held in Las Vegas, the Nevada Athletic Commission was notified of my medical situation. Clearly it was a form of monopoly, and as such, I lost that opportunity. It was devastating for me. Everything I had worked for, everything I had achieved was yanked from beneath me in an instant. Again, it seemed like the world was against me. *How could I overcome so much, so often?*

I had focused and trained hard for the planned fight in the UFC. Since that was no longer an option for me, and yet I was eager to fight again, I took a fight in Shooto versus Yasumi Kohei.

Since my first pro match, I had been bleaching my hair blond. Now I decided to have designs done as well. For the Yasumi fight I had chosen tiger stripes on my head. No one in the sport was really doing things like this at the time. I like to believe I was one of the first to set this trend.

The bell sounded and the fight was on. Yasumi landed the first kick with amazing speed, but I answered that with my own kicks and knees to his midsection. Then we ended up in a long clench as we both tried desperately to get position on one another while moving in and out of position like primal fighters. Yasumi landed a hard knee and nearly knocked the wind out of me. It had hurt, but I didn't want to show any sign of weakness. I grit my teeth and fought on from the clinch. The referee had to break us up several times. We came at each other over and over again, throwing knees and punches and eventually I was able to gain control. Kawaguchi-san (from Shooting Gym Yokohama) was in my corner. In between rounds I heard his voice in my ear. He helped me slow down my breathing and assured me the knee my opponent hit me with had not hurt me. He made me believe my opponent couldn't hurt me. I believed him and stood up from my stool for the final round.

I could tell Yasumi was getting tired. I had an edge over him mentally and had simply beaten his energy out of him. I continued to attack him with kicks and punches, catching him on the tip of his elbow. Pain shot up my leg, but I pushed it away and continued to fight. When the round ended, I recognized the pain again and limped back to my corner. I won that match by decision, and was doubly pleased to see it voted fight of the night.

With the UFC contract having fallen through, even though I continued to fight in Shooto, I was still battling financially. Shooto didn't pay nearly as well as the UFC did. Fight of the night had only won me an extra 10,000 yen or $100 dollars! The fight itself versus Yusumi earned me 150,000 yen ($1,500).

* * * * *

Then came the hammer blow.

On the 27th of March, the year 2001, my father passed away.

I was in a job interview for a position as a business English teacher when I got a call that my father had collapsed.

I can only describe my reaction as that I froze. I didn't know how I was *supposed* to feel; I was simply numb. I just told the interviewers, "I have to go…" and slowly got up to leave the room.

I returned home immediately to be with my father and my mother, who sat by his side. He was pronounced brain dead a few days after suffering a massive stroke. A blood vessel in his neck had burst and blood travelled to his brain. The parallels with the worst scenario for my cyst were all too depressing.

The pronouncement of his death caused my mother to collapse completely. At one point I wondered whether she might even survive that day.

Not terribly religious by nature, I was, however, very accepting and respectful of them. Thus, on that fateful day, I knelt and prayed in the hospital chapel harder than I had ever prayed in my life. Desolate, I felt that my prayers were falling on deaf ears.

Over the following two weeks, with the help of our extended family in Ypsilanti we were focused to come to terms with my father's death. I'd never realized it until it happened but when we were at our weakest, we were forced to make so many important decisions.

Did we want to donate his organs? Will my father's pension be enough for my mother to care for herself? Given her illness, will she be able to care for herself long-term and remain healthy? In hindsight, I wish I had stayed longer to help my mother through one of the most difficult times in her life.

After a heart-felt wake and funeral, my father was buried. We were grateful to have many of his students and close friends in attendance.

I had really wanted my father to see me fight in the UFC, but that never happened.

Following his funeral and my return to Japan, with the help of my manager Kobayashi-san, I took up the refusal to allow me to become a licensed fighter with the New Jersey and Nevada Athletic Commissions. We were prepared to fly out to Las Vegas so they could run all the tests they wanted or needed, but the Nevada Athletic Commission wanted nothing to do with me at that point.

Focusing my efforts on this ordeal with the UFC was my way to avoid grieving my father's death.

The UFC dismissal forced me to seek bookings with rival organizations of the UFC and I did so for the main event in California. It was an event known as King of the Cage. However, the UFC intervened and was able to block me from that event as well. *What the hell is going on?* I thought. *Why am I suddenly being prohibited from doing what I love; doing what I am good at? Doing what I have been doing for so long? Was there some form of conspiracy against me or was it something else—something even more sinister?* I couldn't determine exactly what was going on, but the way it was explained to me by the event owner, Terry Trebilcock, was that the UFC had used blackmail to get their way on this.

Lorenzo and Frank Fertitta were the owners of the UFC and its management company, Zuffa. Lorenzo also used to be on the board of the Nevada Athletic Commission. He retired from it when purchasing the UFC with his brother, but he still had friends in high places.

During this time, the promoters were desperate to promote shows in Las Vegas as it meant big money. "King of the Cage" was told by Zuffa that if they allowed me to fight, Zuffa would make it nearly impossible for the "King of the Cage" to become licensed to promote shows in Vegas.

While this tactic was never proven, as an insider I understood full well how the game was sometimes played. This really put a damper on my future as a mixed martial arts champion and set my life on a crash course that would be devastating to say the least. I had worked so hard for so long and in an instant I was being robbed of my goal!

The UFC rival organization and their event, "King of the Cage 10: Critical Mass" took place on August 4th, 2001.

Denied participation, I continued to fight in Shooto. Needless to say, this turn of events hurt me financially and emotionally. The result was my feeling as though I had hit absolute rock bottom. I couldn't rally my heart and mind after these setbacks.

As a result, I even had a number of losses in much smaller venues. It seemed my fighting career was over and I would never be able to take my skills to that all-important next level—the world stage.

Given everything I had been through, including my father's death, losing my contract with The Ultimate Fighting Championship (UFC) and King of the Cage (KOTC)… I just felt lost. I felt like God, should He exist, was upset with me. Was He punishing me?

Obviously, things could have been considerably worse and

I did have my health, no matter whether the UFC or anyone else would agree. This is something I think I overestimated back then.

I had only one choice—to rebuild myself once again. Ryan Bow would come back harder, smarter, and most definitely stronger.

Naturally, when you work that hard to get the things you want, you also want life to be fair. Unfortunately, it's not... bad things happen to good people.

Chapter Fifteen

Finding a Way to Fight Again

I was desolated and even considered walking away from the sport. Trained as a fighter, I had a deep sense of survival but at one point your intellect kicks in and questions whether you can ultimately win. It didn't matter that I had always dreamed about it as a child and loved it so much. I simply felt defeated and ready to give up. I was disillusioned, heartbroken and frustrated. I would have walked if I hadn't needed the money from the fights. The only emotion stronger than my need to fight was my need to survive.

My father's death lingered over me as a gray cloud that was difficult to ignore. Even today it colors my life as I mourn that my ultimate coach and supporter was not there with me through triumphs.

I kept training and fighting to help release some of the stress and tension. With a sense of defeat, though, my heart just wasn't in it anymore. For a fighter, losing your heart is even worse than fighting without arms and legs. Your heart keeps you fighting when your body has no more strength. It's the magic you call upon when there's no way to win, but you win anyway. That part of me seemed to have drifted away.

It was about that time that I took a job as a bouncer in the Shibuya ward of Tokyo to supplement my income—or lack of it. Bouncing in Japan made me about $1,600 or 160,000 yen per month. I struggled to do everything possible, but still it seemed the universe was against me.

Shibuya was much different than Roppongi. The latter was seen as more of a red light district and foreign clubbing scene, while the equally-crowded clubs of Shibuya catered to a Japan-dominated demographic. I worked at a club named "Womb."

Clubbing never held much interest for me so this was definitely out of my comfort zone. Many clubs in Japan, unlike so many clubs throughout the world, are not smoke-free yet. In fact Womb, like its name, came closer to being a smoker's sanctuary, birthing lung cancer with every breath. The smoke, at times, was unbearable for an athlete like me, but it came with the territory.

In general, bouncers were expected to anticipate troublemakers, confiscate knives or other weapons and patrol the property, inside and out. We seldom worried about guns; unlike the U.S. the Japanese have outlawed them entirely.

Inside, the music loudly blared over the crowded, smoking guests in a scene that was reminiscent of Hades. The club played Techno, House, and Progressive House music. Hip-hop was my preferred music, but I eventually came to like these kinds as well.

We would regularly confiscate drugs like marijuana, ecstasy, and cocaine along with any weapons we might find. When fights did break out, we were there to put a stop to them immediately; occasionally dragging the bullies out kicking and screaming.

I remember one altercation where a *gaijin* decided to chat up a girl. This girl just so happened to be the girlfriend of a member of the notorious *Kanto Rengo* gang. The gang member was understandably pissed when he saw the *gaijin* talking to his girlfriend and things were about to go from bad to worse. Reluctantly with someone of such standing, we had to intervene and ask him to leave. Dealing with gangs is always a dangerous thing even for bouncers due to possible retribution. You never knew whether the gang members might retaliate. We escorted the *Kanto Rengo* gang member and his group from the club and luckily it ended there; or so we hoped.

Eventually I returned to my instincts and needed to get serious again about winning. Coming off that string of losses mid-2001, I decided to charge up my training regime and tried even harder to get my fighting spirit back. I needed to train hard, but I needed to regain that eye of the tiger I'd always had. Put simply, I needed my mojo back.

There was a fitness center called Total Workout—organized by Kohsaka Tsuyoshi and a popular workout facility for top fighters from all over Tokyo. Even to this day I find it strange when fighters say they "need" a cage to train in. At Total Workout, all we had was a hardwood floor similar to the kind used for step aerobics at fitness centers. The floor was covered with thin red puzzle mats and that was the extent of our facility. Being taken down hurt occasionally but, being able to train with many great fighters more than made up for it.

Time-management was a challenge for some of the pros who were unable to make a living fighting. Daytime employment conflicted with the training sessions, but I felt it was critical. Once again I made the sacrifice needed and decided to go without earning money in order to start training with them, although I was still bouncing because it didn't begin until 11 pm. These were always tough decisions for me, but it seemed that even from an early age, I was destined to choose the tougher course.

While training at Total Workout, I trained with the likes of Yoshida Hidehiko, Nakamura Kazuhiro, Lyoto Machida, and Sudo Genki, to name a few. That training group eventually moved when Kohsaka-san opened his own gym called A-Square.

The who's who in MMA always trained at A-Square, so that was the place I wanted to be. Mark Coleman, Phil Baroni and many others trained with us when they were in town from the U.S.

This was when I met Sergio Cunha, the former coach of UFC superstars Anderson Silva and Vanderlei Silva (no relation), at the famous Brazilian gym, Chute Boxe. This chance meeting later led me down a path of greatly improved training techniques and opportunities.

Desiring to improve my striking, in the evenings I trained at Watanabe Boxing Gym into the late hours of the night. I had learned from an early age that success required hard work and dedication, so I used these root ethics to make my comeback and build my strength again. I was able to get some much-needed pad work in with one of the boxing coaches, Hasegawa-san, as well as ring time sparring against several high-caliber pro boxers while I was there. Things were moving along right on schedule and I felt a bit of security in my life creep in.

Chapter Sixteen

9/11

It had been a tough year, but I was beginning to see the light at the end of the tunnel. On September 11th, 2001 I walked in the door after a long day of training. Exhausted, I fell into a chair and flipped on the television to relax…but what I saw caused the opposite. There on the screen was the World Trade Center, on fire. My mother was, at that very moment, in New York City!

She had been visiting one of my cousins on my father's side, Kim, and her husband Robert for a few days. She was scheduled to fly back to Grand Rapids, that day.

In fact, accompanied by family members, my mother had been in route to the airport in Newark, New Jersey. As they drove down the highway, they could see smoke off in the distance, but had no clue what had happened.

By the time they reached the airport, it was clear that something was very, very wrong. The airport was literally closed; in lockdown. No one could get out or in.

* * * * *

My aunt, Donna, was a flight attendant for Northwest Airlines. It was supposed to be an easy day for her. She left Detroit at 6:30 am on that fateful day and arrived safely in Newark. She was scheduled to return to Detroit at 9:30 am on another flight, but it flight would be delayed. She was locked inside the airport at the time it all went down. Instead, she watched from the airport window as the second plane crashed into the World Trade Center. She witnessed it with her own eyes!

With a cold fear, she realized that her sister, my mother, was due to arrive at the airport at any time. She cried hysterically as she tried to contact her. It would be a several hours before they were able to reach each other on the phone. My mother had returned to Kim and Robert's home. She would need to find another way to get home. Mom called me as soon as she could, knowing I would be worried!

At that time, I had no clue how bad it really was. I was able to speak and write Japanese, but I was still learning. There was a lot I still didn't understand. When I awakened the next morning, it was all over newspapers; even in Japan. Worried, I met with my manager, Kobayashi-san, and she explained to me in simple Japanese so I could understand the severity of the situation.

It wasn't until I was finally able to reach my mother that I was able to calm down. She was safe! Instead of flying, she rode the Greyhound bus 16 hours to Detroit where Kim's mother and father, my Aunt Germaine and Uncle David, gave her a ride back to Grand Rapids.

Donna returned safely to Detroit later that night by plane.

Terrorist attacks in America? I was relieved to be in a far away land, but my heart went out to those whose lives were affected.

On October 8th that year, I was asked to compete in "Contenders," a grappling event put on by WK Network. This would be a first for me because no strikes were allowed. It was grappling only. I was matched up against Komuro Koji, a well-known Japanese Judoka (judo competitor).

As I approached the match, I was nowhere near as nervous as I was in MMA fights. That might have been due to the certainty that I wouldn't be—couldn't be, knocked out. The risk of injury was not nearly so great.

Komuro was known for being very good at a move he called the *komu lock*. The komu lock is a version of the judo technique, *sode-guruma-jime*. It is also known as the Ezequiel choke. The technique compresses the opponent's trachea or the carotid arteries. It can be executed from a variety of positions, but is generally performed by wrapping one arm behind the opponent's head and grasping onto the sleeve of the *gi* (uniform) with the opposite hand.

In order to avoid it, I took him down with a double leg takedown and quickly passed his guard into side position. He replaced his guard and slowed the pace of the match down by repeatedly trying to apply the *komu lock*. I was content to stay out of harm's way. Round one ended with me in his guard.

I began to get a little frustrated in round two. Komuro was wearing a judo uniform; a *gi* and it became more challenging to use my speed against him. After avoiding the *komu lock* again, I was able to create some distance, pass his guard, and take his back. Thus came my chance to end it.

I extended my legs and applied pressure to his lower back to take his base away. As time ran out in the final round, I applied a rear naked choke. The round ended before Komuro tapped out. I won on the judge's scorecard.

In a solemn salute to those who died on 9/11, I stood on the ropes and raised the American flag. The response was a cheer from the crowd. It was a small gesture, but I wanted the media, as well as the world, to know that I was praying for them.

Chapter Seventeen

I Have Arrived

It was March of 2002 when I would earn the number one spot in the Shooto world rankings. All my hard work was finally paying off. The fight versus Cromado earned me 300,000 yen or $3,000.

The fight that carried me there was against the well-known Marcio Cromado. The skilled Brazilian fighter had recently come off a win choking the Shooto Welterweight Title Holder, Uno Kaoru, unconscious in a non-title bout.

Uno Kaoru fought out of the gym, Wajutsu Keishukai; a gym I still trained at from time to time. Cromado then choked out another ranked Shooto Welterweight, Nakayama Takumi. With a win, Cromado would have earned himself a real title shot with Uno Kaoru again. However, my win changed his plans.

By this time, despite the difficulties of being a foreigner in Japan, I was pretty well known. It wasn't uncommon to be stopped on the street and asked for pictures or an autograph.

This also led to other opportunities, in and outside the ring. I had the opportunity to do a little modeling and appeared on a few Japanese television shows. Normally, these shows are filmed in advance. However, "O Rei Do Shooto" aired live as we filmed it.

I was the topic. Fans were invited to draw a picture of me and the winner would receive a prize. Near the end of the show, we'd received several replies. I chose a winner while we were still live on television and they won several items including t-shirts and other memorabilia. How my life had changed!

The majority of my fights were aired on television in Japan by this time. It wasn't uncommon to have the media present while I trained. I really had to concentrate not to lose focus with a camera on me constantly during training sessions, and giving interviews before and after took some getting used to.

Gradually I grew more accustomed to the media and fans. After all, it was part of my job as a fighter; I was an entertainer and it was a spectator sport.

I have to say it certainly was fun at times but, at the same time, was tiring. While I wouldn't say that I deliberately avoided being in the public, it did eventually become more comfortable to watch an event from the comfort of my home rather than in person at the arena. When I did go to the arena to watch, I spent most of my time backstage.

I think this is why I've grown more private than I was as a youngster. I prefer quite times with a few good friends over crowded places.

* * * * *

The business of fighting in Japan is different than in some other parts of the world. In this sense, being "the local guy" is not exactly an asset.

What many people don't realize is that in the Japanese fight scene, even in the big events, the majority of Japanese fighters are not paid anywhere near as much as their foreign opponents. Foreign fighters who live abroad were usually paid in cash; even with large sums, immediately after the event. Meanwhile, Japanese, and other fighters like myself residing in Japan, were paid via electric funds transfer into our bank accounts up to 30 days after the event.

From that perspective, speaking Japanese and trying to do things the "Japanese way" actually worked against me. The event promoters knew I spoke Japanese and that I had earned my spot within the organization just as Japanese fighters did; by fighting my way up the rankings. Thus, they were able to justify the difference in pay because we were not well known abroad. They even expected that we be good "company men" (and women) and not speak up or fight for equal pay. In Japan, "the nail that sticks out, gets hammered down" so to speak.

* * * * *

By this point I had known Enson for a while, just by association. I wouldn't go so far as to say we were close, but we saw each other around town from time to time and would exchange polite glances.

A mutual friend, Todd, had mentioned to Enson that I might have been interested in a job. This was perfect timing because Enson was planning to open Purebred Tokyo "Killer Bee" in the upcoming months. He needed people. People like *me*!

So in November of 2002, Enson offered me a job at his new gym. Despite my recent success, I was still struggling financially at the time. So I took the job. I ran "Killer Bee" in Tokyo alongside Japanese superstar, Yamamoto "Kid" Norifumi.

Enson required "Kid" or "Nori" as we called him, live in the gym. He slept on a Japanese futon on the floor in the office. I think this was done to motivate Kid to improve his lifestyle and stay out of trouble.

Kid was a talented athlete. His father was an Olympic wrestler and both his sisters (Yamamoto) Miyu and Seiko were also champions in wrestling, so it was more or less a family legacy.

Slower days often consisted of hanging around the gym, talking, and just having fun. We did most of our training in the evening after teaching various classes for the general public.

Enson had also employed a tattoo artist. Takumi tattooed many of Enson's fighters. I had one of my tattoos actually done right at the gym during business hours. Takumi brought all of his equipment and got to work on my tattoo. I got a version of the words that many of Enson's fighters had: *Yamato Damashii* or Japanese Fighting Spirit. I had it incorporated on my left arm into a Koi Fish design with the Koi swimming upstream to symbolize "battling with great perseverance to reach the top."

There was a basis to the symbolism of the koi. There is an age-old tale wherein the koi are said to have climbed a waterfall, undaunted by the lunging current. Their perseverance paid off; an achievement that required great determination. I could identify with this.

I love Japanese tattoo art because it is detail-oriented and the symbolism of each design adds to its aura. That said, the sound of the needle going in and out of the skin is hard to get used to. It can be fairly painful, depending on the location and amount of time it takes to complete it; with directly on bone hurting the most.

Enson had taken Kid in after he had been kicked out of college due to an altercation involving the Yakuza. He had been wrestling at college and when he couldn't do that anymore, he decided to try his hand at Shooto. He adapted to the rules quickly and won the All Japan Amateur Shooto Championship. After that he turned pro immediately.

It was during my time running this gym that I got my first real taste of the darker side of Japan.

* * * * *

The gym where I was working was owned in part or sponsored by two *Yakuza* members. The *Yakuza* are Japan's equivalent to the mafia. I recall hearing them scream and threaten people over the phone on numerous occasions. Apparently many of those people owed them money and just like their counterparts in America; it was either pay up or swim with the fishes.

This coincided with a period when the Japanese and Chinese mafias were at war with each other. Both partners were members of the *Yakuza* group, *Inagawa-kai*. This branch of the *Yakuza* claims a membership of over 80,000 and is actually recognized, but regulated, under Japanese organized crime control laws.

One of the sponsors we called: *Eiji-san*. *Eiji* was his first name with *san* used as a term of respect. Japanese people are generally referred to by their last name. I think he told me his name was *Eiji* because I'm American.

I'm not able to recall the other partner's name. Neither was tall or particularly muscular; therefore non-threatening in the purely physical sense. However, Eiji's eyes were dark and carried a depth of angry temper.

The other partner came off more as a "happy, well-mannered" kind of person. Eiji was 30. The other sponsor was roughly 34. Both men's backs were covered in traditional tattoos. This is a sure sign that they were *Yakuza*.

Each day they came to the gym accompanied by two bodyguards. One was a big foreigner, muscular but also over-weight, and the other, Japanese. He seemed to be in good shape.

Both sponsors lived in very nice, expensive homes in Tokyo and drove brand new Mercedes Benz.

We were paid in cash only. I guess I was naïve at the time because I do remember thinking it odd that we did not receive a pay stub, etc. It was definitely all done "under the table".

It was common to see our sponsors be accompanied by their bodyguards; there was evidently a fear of assassination. I guess that came with the territory of their chosen lifestyle.

One day when Kid and I were sitting in the gym talking about fights of the previous weekend, the darker side of Japan reared its ugly head.

Kid got a call from his sister, Miyu, saying that Iseno "Ise" Toshikazu had been jumped by a gang and had been badly hurt to the point of requiring surgery. Kid rushed to be by Ise's side while I stayed at the gym to run things. Enson was out of town on business at the time so he couldn't be there to calm Kid down.

In his absence, our *Yakuza* sponsors had intervened and had demanded that the families of the kids that hurt Ise pay money for the attack. That's right—they were going to extort them for money. They almost succeeded.

Before they closed the deal, Kid and a group of his friends jumped the other gang, beating them severely. They had taken their revenge. This beating cancelled out the extortion and all deals were off. It's amazing how in Japan this kind of stuff never really makes it into the mainstream news.

Then there was the altercation I witnessed that involved Enson, himself. Enson, the team and I had just arrived at Korakuen Hall. As we made our way backstage, a Japanese businessman approached Enson. He proceeded to greet Enson, but this angered Enson immensely.

As it was later explained to me, the guy was currently suing the sponsor of Purebred Kyoto, another one of Enson's gyms. The sponsor of the Kyoto gym was also a *Yakuza* member. It had angered Enson that the guy was acting as if nothing was wrong.

I'm not sure was transpired next, but after watching part of the event out on the main floor, I returned backstage to see the same man literally on his hands and knees begging for Enson's forgiveness. Kid had to hold Enson back because he was ready to rip the guy apart. Eventually Enson calmed down and let the guy go.

Situations like these were not the norm, but definitely not something I had expected. This was a part of Japan I had not yet seen; in fact, many Japanese never witness situations like these.

Chapter Eighteen

Looking for Normal

As life went on, and since I wasn't training all the time, I had more opportunity for normal life and things like dating. Up to this point, I had only dated Japanese women. I would, however, eventually meet and marry an American woman whom I met in Japan.

Many foreigners come to Japan and fall in love with Japanese women due to their differences. The longer you live in Japan you begin to see what can sometimes set the tone for relationships between Japanese and *gaijin*. In many cases, this will be accompanied by the stigma of one wanting to be seen with the other in public; a sort of status symbol. This happens because Japanese who are willing to date foreigners, more specifically, native English speakers, are equally interested in improving their English ability as they are in the relationship itself.

In my opinion, this gave relationships an awkward and unnatural beginning.

As the koi who always swims against the current, I still wanted be accepted as an equal; not someone's personal English teacher. By this time, I was fluent in Japanese. It had become easier to express myself in Japanese than English, as that was the culture I had come to identify with more and more.

This is part of the reason that I chose to date an American woman instead. I found comfort in someone who did not view me as an outsider or different, but shared similar views in life.

Her name was Angie and she taught English full-time but also worked part-time as a hostess. In Japan, a hostess will

117

sit in a lounge-type setting and pour alcohol while talking with Japanese businessmen.

Angie dated mostly Japanese men prior to meeting me and although we were both Americans, we spoke Japanese to each other during those first few months we were together.

As things became more serious, I asked her to quit her part-time job as a hostess. I believed that between the two of us, we had more than enough money to support ourselves. As it turned out, I was wrong.

At the time we were living in Kichijoji, a popular, leafy western suburb of Musashino, Tokyo. We lived in a nice *mansion*, a 3 story concrete apartment building. It was a 2LDK; 2 bedrooms, living room, dining room and kitchen. It had nice hard wood floors and for the first time in years, I slept in a proper bed, instead of a futon on the floor. We were paying 130,000 yen or $1,300 between the two of us.

* * * * *

On June 8th 2003, I ended up facing a muay thai kickboxing champion named Miyake Yuji. In the ring, he went by the name "Hayato."

I say "ended up" because I was not a kickboxer; I was a mixed martial artist. Our Yakuza sponsors were very enthusiastic about the sport, but they knew little to nothing about choosing the right fights for us. They were adamant about me fighting, so I decided to try my hand at kickboxing and hopefully not embarrass myself in the process. After all, I had just become the number one world ranked Shooto fighter.

In order to prepare, I decide to train in Thailand so I could focus solely on muay thai. Ise had just recovered from surgery after being jumped so, Enson asked him to accompany me.

I was excited to return to Thailand to train. We arrived during the three-day Songkran festival, The Thai New Year Festival. The Thais celebrate the New Year from the 13th to

118

the 15th of April. While the holiday is observed throughout the country, the biggest celebrations take place in the northern city of Chiang Mai. A favorite for visiting foreigners, the holiday is celebrated for six days and sometimes even longer. One of the unique gestures of celebration includes the Thais roaming the city streets with water guns or containers of water, which they use to soak people who pass by. Overall, it is a time for family and particularly to respect the elders.

Since training wouldn't begin until the following day, we spent one night in Bangkok to enjoy the festival. The next day we took a taxi to the former Lumpini Champion, Santien Noi's, gym to begin training. It was located just north of Bangkok in the province of Pathum Thani.

The gym was dirty and seemed harsh, but it got the job done. We slept sixteen guys to a room under mosquito nets and manually flushed toilets by pouring water over the waste. We showered outside using a basin of water and a small bucket. Cows and fighting chickens were kept on the gym grounds as well. Most would be surprised at the conditions we were forced to endure, but it was some of the best muay thai training I've ever had. We trained twice a day every day and after a while didn't even notice how hard it was just to brush our teeth.

I returned from Thailand in great shape. I knew muay thai wasn't my strong point, but I felt good about my chances.

The fight took place at a club named Velfarre in Tokyo. It was being sponsored by Ikusa, a kickboxing company I knew very little about. The only thing I knew was that Hayato was their star and they wanted him to beat me!

Hayato was significantly taller than me and it showed when we met in the ring. I was the aggressor in round one. As soon as the bell sounded, I attacked with a rush of punches. One thing I'd learned in Thailand was that my kicks were not as good as they needed to be for this fight. My plan was to draw him close and make him trade punches with me.

Things seemed to be going as planned. Every time he'd get close to me I'd fire strong punches at him. I countered every kick he threw with a left hook or right straight. Hayto began to catch on to my game plan and every time I got close enough to throw punches, he would clinch me and counter my punches with strong knees to my midsection.

Round one ended and I couldn't believe it! We were only one round in and I was already beginning to get tired. Kickboxing was definitely out of my comfort zone and it was showing.

I managed to recover enough to look fresh for round two. I stuck to my game plan and continued to stay active by answering each one of his kicks with a punch. That's when it happened.

Just as he prepared to fire a left kick to my ribs, I landed a big left hook that floored him. The crowd went wild! They hadn't expected that. I hadn't either! Hayato was able to stand up before the referee counted to ten. I rushed him with a barrage of punches and tried to finish the fight, but couldn't land any clean punches.

Hayato managed to recover. He could tell that I'd worn myself out. He tried to make a comeback and had started to land several kicks and knees. I felt a hard knee land and heard a crack. He'd cracked one of my ribs with one of his knees. Luckily, the round ended.

In the third and final round, I sucked it up and fought on. We traded punches and kicks non-stop in the last round; each of us trying our best to win the fight. The gong sounded and the fight was over. All three judges scored the bout in my favor. I'd done the impossible. I'd beaten a kickboxing champion at his own game. This fight versus Hayato earned me 300,000 yen or $3,000; good pay at the time for kickboxing outside of the K-1 organization.

* * * * *

And then things started really getting bad. I was being

told I was about to be deported from Japan for issues with my Visa. The Yakuza sponsors had promised to sponsor my visa, but they dropped the ball and I was about to pay for it big time.

It seemed my whole world was crashing down around me again and I was powerless to do anything about it. For the first time in my life, things were beginning to feel hopeless. This seemed to be a fight I couldn't win with my fists but one I still needed to overcome. It's one thing when they beat your body; it's something else when you let them conquer your soul. I wasn't going to let that happen. I had come too far in life to be defeated now. I thought it would be wise to distance myself from Purebred Tokyo "Killer Bee" and the *Yakuza*. So that's what I did.

By leaving Killer Bee I was also forced to seek work elsewhere. I had gotten used to a more comfortable lifestyle; a lifestyle that didn't require me to work on the side, so at this point I had no choice but to go back to teaching English. I found a part-time job at a small English school named "T.I.E. - Think In English" in the illustrious Ginza district of Tokyo.

T.I.E. was on the sixth floor of an old building; one that came alive when the earthquakes struck. Earthquakes are very much a part of everyday life in Japan. You come to accept and learn to live with them. Once every hundred years or so, a massive earthquake hits Tokyo. It is not a matter of *if* it will happen, but a matter of *when*.

One day I remember going over a student's homework with them when the building started to shake violently, swaying back and forth. It was a frightening experience, but I had learned to simply ride them out. That is, after all, your only real choice.

Amazingly, many Japanese buildings will remain standing while actually swaying back and forth. The Japanese have learned to build flexibility into their structures for this very reason. Indeed, some engineers have managed to accomplish structures that will actually bend in half and then retain that altered shape, but will not break. The Japanese have also long investigated options for predicting quakes. There is some evidence that their famous koi fish exhibit erratic behavior just before a quake; theoretically because the water provides an advance sense of vibration over land. While escape from the Japanese islands is not practical, at least choosing appropriate shelter could potentially save many lives.

Teaching English was just a means to an end for me, and Angie knew this. When I was training for a fight, I rarely had time to teach English. Luckily, as sporadic as it often was, when I did fight, I made more money than I had early on in my career. Angie was supportive of my fighting career at this point in our relationship, but I didn't know how long that would last. The life of a fighter can be very difficult on a relationship, even the strongest ones. With my decision to leave Purebred Tokyo, we decided to move closer to another one of Enson's gyms.

Some years earlier Enson had purchased the Super Tiger Gym, the place where I had made my amateur debut. The gym was now called "Purebred Omiya."

Angie and I chose to live in Koshigaya City, Saitama Prefecture. Moving out of the big city enabled us to get a bigger mansion for a lower price.

We lived in a 3LDK; a 3 bedroom apartment with a living room, dining room and kitchen. Again, it had hardwood floors and we paid 110,000 yen or $1,100 per month between the two of us.

Profiling does not only happen in the U.S. In Japan, unfortunately, it's one of the "perks" of being a *gaijin*. Because shortly after we moved in, one evening Angie had gone to a store nearby to buy a few things. As she walked home, she noticed that the police were following her. They stopped her and demanded to see her ID. She didn't have it on her because it was late and she hadn't planned on being gone very long. Despite her explanation, they brought her home in the police car; still demanding to see her paperwork. When she arrived home, she was crying hysterically. She wanted to know why the police were bothering her.

Angie had a working visa in Japan and being stopped by the police was a first for her—unlike me. I was angered to hear what had happened and I followed her outside to talk with the police.

I am a calm person by nature, but I was on the verge of screaming. I was angered by their treatment and the officers could tell. I think they thought I might over-react and create a situation, but eventually I calmed down. She showed them her ID (*gaijin card*) and they apologized and went on their way. Legally working and residing in Japan, we couldn't catch a break.

That being said, I had yet to find a solution for my ongoing visa problems and time was running out. I was going to go from being legally employed to illegally employed very soon if I didn't figure something out....

Chapter Nineteen

Politics and Preservation

Enson caught a lot of heat for his outrageous escapades like beating up paparazzi, being involved with the Yakuza and just his outspoken manner. I can truly say, however, that when the chips were down, he took good care of me.

I remember it like it was yesterday; he reached into his pocket and handed me the keys to his apartment in Thailand, where he would regularly visit, taking fighters with him to train muay thai.

I had received an official notice from the Tokyo immigration bureau that my visa would not be renewed. I had two weeks to leave the country or I would be deported.

I spent the following two weeks back in Bangkok wandering around until Enson and the gym could figure out a way to get me my visa for Japan. This was the second time I'd done this over the previous six months. Luckily, they were able to help me obtain an entertainment visa in August of 2003, so for the moment, things seemed better.

Having left Purebred Tokyo, I no longer had the *Yakuza* sponsors. I was out of a job and was not getting the high profile fights I needed. The money I made from teaching English helped, but it wasn't enough. I was beginning to question and doubt everything, all the while wondering how long it would be until things improved.

Despite these difficulties, Angie and I were married on the idyllic north shore of Hawaii on September 23rd, 2004. In hindsight, we were in no position financially to get married.

Angie and I argued quite a bit over how we would marry. Knowing that times were hard, I wanted to file the paperwork at the city office and have the wedding we wanted at a later date. My other suggestion was to come up with a budget we could afford and have the wedding in Japan.

Traditionally in Japan, when you get married, instead of gifts, you receive *oshugi* or "celebration money." Getting married in Japan would have certainly lightened our financial load.

Instead, we chose Hawaii so our families could attend. I understood, but I wish we had been able to agree upon a budget for it. Angie had dreamed about her wedding day since she was a little girl. Everything had to be perfect. We spent so much on the wedding that it eventually created marital issues.

Married life was a constant struggle. Despite our love, Angie and I had two very different views on how to save or spend money. I had become accustomed to not having much over the years. Angie, on the other hand, had been used to having plenty of money in Japan. She had been a top-earning hostess for a short period of time so she was used to having nice things. My suggested budget didn't sit well with her. As a fighter, a budget is crucial because you never know when your next payday will come or when you might get injured. This made a compatible life together nearly impossible.

* * * * *

By this time, the popularity of Shooto had started to fade and I had just barely come up short; losing in the finals of the Shooto Pacific Rim Tournament to Boku Kotetsu. A life and an income as a mixed martial arts fighter has no certainties. I had earned $3,000 or 300,000 yen versus Boku.

With hopes of having a reliable source of income, in April of 2005 I opened up my own gym in Japan called "Kaminari Dojo." With an introduction by Toida Katsuya from Wajutsu Keishukai, I was able to come to an agreement with Gold's Gym, Japan in order to use their facility. Kaminari Dojo at Gold's Gym earned me about 100,000 yen or $1,000 monthly. I taught four days a week for 90 minutes.

I started Kaminari Dojo, with Enson's blessing while fighting for and representing Purebred Omiya. I didn't have any students experienced enough to help me train for the fights, so I returned to the group at A-Square to prepare for them.

Having met coach Sergio Cunha before and since, I trained at A-Square alongside Olympic gold medalist and Pride fighter Yoshida Hidehiko. Then, I was invited to train at Yoshida's gym, "Yoshida Dojo" in 2007, where Sergio Cunha had been hired as the MMA coach. At that time, they were the only ones in Japan doing the same things the American gyms had recently started doing, which was hiring some of the best coaches available to better their athletes.

The Yoshida Dojo fighters were all former elite level *judoka*. They were employed by a management company called "J-Rock" and received a salary to train and fight. That was much different than how it worked for other fighters, like myself, who fought from paycheck to paycheck and were only rewarded when we fought.

I learned so much about training under Cunha at Yoshi Dojo. Initially, with his help, I had hopes of being brought on as one of their professional athletes. However, despite Cunha personally introducing me and requesting that I be brought onto the team, J-Rock decided not to hire me.

I had been up against the odds before in my life, in fact on many occasions, so after months of soul searching I decided to find a way back to being able to support myself competing in the sport that I loved so much. I decided to find a way to win again in the ring of Shooto or any other organization where I could find an "in." After all, I was a warrior; not a quitter.

With the help of an American-based Japanese MMA Agent, Hirata Shu, I signed with a promotion company named "BodogFight" and fought one fight in Costa Rica on February 17, 2007. I was excited. This was the first time one of my fights would air on TV in America. After all these years my family and friends in America would finally be able to see what I did first-hand.

I spent two weeks in Costa Rica filming season four of BodogFight. The flight was a long one. After a 14-hour trip from Narita Airport, we (the other Japanese fighters who would be competing, our corner men, and I) landed in Texas. From there, it was another three-hour flight to San Jose, Costa Rica. We spent one night at a small hotel in San Jose before continuing on our journey.

As the capital of Costa Rica, the city is home to more than a third of the entire country's population. Costa Rica shares a discovery history with the U.S. in that Christopher Columbus was first to sink a foreign flag. Costa Rica has a much stronger Spanish influence, however, which is particularly evident in the architecture of its theatres, museums, homes and other governmental buildings.

Since San Jose is landlocked at the center of the country, the next morning, we took a two-hour bus ride to the coast, and then a huge cruise ship to the location where we would be filming. It would all be held at the Barcelo Hotel in Tambor, Costa Rica.

Perhaps it was the "all you can eat" hotel buffets that got the best of me, as I had to cut seventeen pounds to make weight for the fight this time around. After almost twenty hours of hard dieting and training, I made weight.

It was difficult to maintain a good training regimen. Due to the filming schedule for television, my corner man, Kunioku Kiuma, and I trained from 6-8 am. Kunioklu is a former Pancrase World Champion and having him in my corner was helpful.

As one of the mixed martial arts companies, Pancrase was founded in 1993 by professional wrestlers Masakatsu Funaki and Minoru Suzuki. Based on pankration, which was a sport from the original Olympic Games, these athletes were particularly skilled in catch wrestling thus molding their promotion around professional wrestling and shoots rather than works. As in Japanese professional wrestling, closed-fisted punches were not permitted to the head, but are allowed to the body. The fighter may instead strike with a palm and the holds must break when the competitor makes it to the ropes.

Training had to be early because immediately afterwards, we were taken all over the place to film. I remember filming a promo for the event. The film crew asked a family with young children who obviously could use extra money to use their rural home to film.

Kunioku held mitts for me in what could be considered their kitchen as I punched and kicked the mitts for the camera.

Cutting the weight had left me so exhausted that I had to receive an IV from one of the event physicians immediately after weigh-ins; just 24 hours before the fight, to replace the electrolytes I had lost.

The fight took place in a ring on the beach, about thirty yards from the water. The whole experience was very different for me.

The event was held at 9 am. I use the word "event" loosely because other than the other fighters and corner men, there was virtually no crowd or spectators. As a fighter, hearing excitement in the crowd can help keep you focused; help you continue to fight when things get rough. The lack of a crowd was a first for me.

My opponent was Nick Agallar, a 5'8" 155 lb. fighter from the Freestyle Fighting Academy. This Racine, Wisconsin native came out throwing heavy punches in the first round. I traded punches with him for a short time and then he suddenly shot in and got a double leg takedown on me. I clamped on a guillotine chokehold as he shot in but he was able to escape. Then he passed my guard, eventually mounting me and gaining the upper hand. All I saw was fists of fury raining down on my head like a battering ram. He forced me to give him my back, which is an even more dangerous and vulnerable position to be in. Once I was on my back he continued to throw punches to the sides of my head and they felt like hammers. I was trapped and I knew it and was unable to escape. I endured a lot of punishment during that first round and was relieved to hear the sound of the bell at the end of it.

I remember the whisper of defeat in between rounds. In Japan, I was, more often than not, physically stronger than my opponents. This time I'd found myself in a battle of wills with someone physically stronger than I. I had to find a way to win, despite this.

My opponent and I touched gloves to begin round two. He immediately started throwing punches at my head. This is what many consider to be unsportsmanlike conduct; throwing punches almost instantly after we touched gloves.

Using his punches to force me to guard my face, he shot in for the takedown. I attempted the guillotine chokehold on him again as I did in round one. This time I got it and it was tight. After just a few seconds my opponent tapped out.

Nick was rumored to have a multi-fight deal with BodogFight that had him earning $20,000 per fight. I hoped with a win over him, I could receive a similar deal. The fight versus Nick Agallar earned me $8,000 in total including a $2,000 bonus I received for "Comeback of the Season" for season four of BodogFight.

I returned to Japan, victorious, shortly thereafter.

Chapter Twenty

Wedding Ring vs. Fighting Ring

In my absence, Angie had taken the time to reflect on our relationship and more importantly, her life. One day shortly after my return, she turned to me and simply said, "I think I'm bisexual…"

This was an immense shock for me, but perhaps not for reasons you may be thinking. Angie grew up in a very religious family; a very strict Christian family. Growing up, she did not cut her hair and had not participated in gym class because it would require her to wear shorts. As she grew older, she did not even wear makeup. She was the girl who spoke in tongues, on occasion, in church.

Once she moved to Japan and met people from all walks of life, she became more open-minded, religiously speaking. For example, it is said "Japanese are born Shinto, marry Christian, and die Buddhist." These refer to the pivotal points in life. However, when asked, most Japanese will say they are *mushuukyou*, "without religion."

At first, I'm sure this was something that conflicted with her original beliefs. But, as time went on and she met a lot of really kind people, her views became more open.

Angie wanted to explore these thoughts of bisexuality she was having. This was hard to hear for me; not the part about her possibly being bisexual, though. In my mind, our marriage vows and its inherent monogamy were sacred. There was no room for another person, no matter who they were. Our decision was based on each other as human beings—not being male or female. Our vows trumped everything in my eyes.

* * * * *

131

I desperately wanted to stay active and to take my mind off what was going on at home. I signed to fight with an organization named "Deep" – a respected organization known to send fighters who performed well in their events to Pride, the biggest event in the world at the time, trumping even the UFC.

Deep is a Japanese mixed martial arts promoting and sanctioning organization. It is promoted by Saeki Shigeru, who is also the former public relations director of Pride Fighting Championships. Their inaugural event took place in 2001 and featured Paulo Filho and Royler Gracie.

Deep started playing the role of subcontractor for Pride Fighting Championships since Dream Stage Entertainment (DSE) started promoting Pride Bushido events which focused on fighters at middleweight and lightweight in September 2003. For this reason, many Japanese fighters chose to fight in events promoted by Deep instead of other Japanese promotions. For instance, Chonan Ryo and Minowa Ikuhisa (Minowaman) are an example of fighters that became famous because of Deep.

Thus, I was set to fight at Korakuen Hall on April 13th, 2007. My opponent would be Tomioka Yoshihiro, also known as "Barbaro 44." He was a 161 lb. welterweight from Japan.

After weigh-ins the night before the fight, I must have eaten something bad because I developed food poisoning. I hoped it would pass by the next morning, but awoke to find myself still having stomach cramps. I spent the day in bed, hoping the pain would ease up, but it didn't. I would be forced to fight through it.

Despite the stomach cramps and misery I was in, I slowly made my way to the ring when my name was announced. All I could think of was that I just wanted to get it over with.

The first two rounds of the fight went on pretty much as expected as we traded punches and kicks in the center of the ring, But, I had grown very tired going into round three. I knew the fight was close, so I needed to suck it up. My best chance of winning was to secure the takedown and do some major damage from the top position. I was weak from the poisoning and perspiration sheeted my brow and burned my eyes.

I quickly shot in and got the takedown. I was able to land punches from within his guard, body-body-head, over and over again. I punched him hard to the body first to get him to lower his guard and when he did, and attacked his head vehemently. I think at this point I was operating on pure instinct—original strategy was not an option.

Barbaro eventually scrambled to his feet and tried to regain his senses. I heard my corner scream, "Take him down again!" so I pushed him up against the ropes and scored another quick takedown. Barbaro immediately tried to scurry back to his feet again, but I knew I had him at that point. During the scramble I was able to take his back and secure the rear naked choke. That did the trick and he tapped out.

My fight against Barbaro 44 should have earned me a title shot. In fact, after the referee raised my hand, I addressed the crowd in Japanese. I expressed my gratitude. Without their cheers, I may not have been able to put aside how sick I was feeling. Next, I looked directly at the founder of Deep himself, Saeki-san and asked for a title shot. The crowd applauded with their acceptance.

In the upcoming months, I would find out that Deep had decided against it. My reward was only to be the 500,00 yen ($5,000) purse. It was simply very hard – and very emblematic of – being a *gaijin*.

I decided to take another offer that was on the table. BodogFight had finally made me an offer for a multi-fight contract. Although not as lucrative as I'd hoped following my win over Nick Agallar, it paid more than fighting in Japan.

(1st fight: $8,000, 2nd fight $10,000, 3rd fight $12,000. My pay would increase as long as I won.) I remember this time in my life particularly well because my marriage had hit rock bottom and as a result, I couldn't stop feeling like my world was closing in on me.

Here was my best chance to be able to fully provide for my family again. There was, however, one obstacle. If I was going to fight the best, I needed to get the best training possible. So my wife and I decided to move back to San Jose so I could train at the famed American Kickboxing Academy (AKA); the same gym where I'd turned pro all those years earlier under Frank Shamrock.

But by that June of 2007, Frank was no longer a part of the gym. However, AKA still had many of the best fighters in the world, meaning I could train alongside Cain Velasquez, Jon Fitch, Josh Koscheck, Luke Rockhold, and Josh Thomson.

I moved to San Jose a couple months early to prepare for my upcoming fight. I spent the first month renting a room at AKA's MMA Coach "Crazy" Bob Cook's house. He lived just a few miles from the gym so this made commuting easy. I shared a room with Cain Velasques. Cain would go on to become the UFC Heavyweight Champion a few years later.

I slept on an air mattress. Although it was a definite improvement over my days at the *gaijin house* in Yokohama, Japan, I had become used to sleeping in a bed after my marriage to Angie. Sleeping on an air mattress made it hard to recover after countless hours of hard training.

I spent the little spare time I had to look for an apartment for Angie and I to live in when she arrived. It had been decided that I would move ahead and she would follow. I realized that this was a big adjustment for us and wanted to make sure she was comfortable. Eventually, I was able to find a small but nice apartment near the gym. I signed the six-month lease and prepared for Angie's arrival.

Angie was looking forward to living in the Bay area when

I left her in Japan. She regularly belly danced and practiced yoga, and was excited to learn more since the Bay area had many very good schools for both.

As the time for her departure neared, however, she had a drastic change of heart. She decided to remain in Japan. I was absolutely devastated.

To this day, I am not sure what caused this sudden change of heart. Had she grown tired of my endeavors and the stress it placed on our relationship? Or was it this newly found desire to explore bisexuality? It didn't matter; the result was the same. I managed to cancel the apartment lease and then, once again, I was on my own.

My fight in BodogFight did not go as planned. I had trained hard and had a great team backing me. Mentally, I was a mess.

The fight took place in Vancouver, British Columbia in August of 2007. I hadn't seen Angie in several months. A training partner from AKA and a friend from Japan were in town for the event as well. I chose to have them corner me so that I could have my wife flown to Vancouver for the event.

In hindsight, this was a terrible idea. We had been arguing consistently and when she arrived, it continued. We could not agree on the simplest detail and the stress was enormous. I had trained so hard for this fight, but all I could think about was trying to talk to Angie in-depth about our problems.

* * * * *

My opponent was the two-time Brazilian jiu-jitsu champion from Brazil, Rodrigo Damm.

I expected Rodrigo to want to take the fight to the ground so, my plan was to keep it standing. There was no need to fight to his strengths.

I was able to keep the fight standing in round one. Toward the end, I'd clipped him with a good punch and forced him to try to take me down. I defended the takedown successfully and the round ended. I thought to myself, *despite everything*

135

that's going on in my life, I have to set it aside and win! My livelihood depended on it; *our* livelihood depended on it.

Round two started and I stuck to my game plan. I don't actually remember what happened next, but I must have lowered my hands to defend the takedown for a second. My opponent took advantage of my mistake and threw a huge over-hand right (punch). It landed flush and I went down. Rodrigo rushed in to finish the fight and the referee stopped it. I pleaded with him to let me continue, but he'd decided I had had enough.

Having no peripheral vision out of either eye on my left side had finally caught up with me once again. This was quite different from a teenager's car accident—this would affect the rest of my life.

BodogFight folded almost immediately afterwards, which meant I lost my multi-fight contract.

* * * * *

I returned to Tokyo in September of 2007 at the age of 28. Things had escalated between Angie and I to the point that we decided to live separately.

This time I rented a studio apartment in Denenchoufu City, Tokyo with the hope that a little more time apart would help us figure out what were going to do; if we were meant to be together or not. Angie and I had grown apart. It was as if she had finally found herself and could no longer see a future with me.

A few months later, we decided to officially separate. We mutually agreed that we would start dating other people. She had become a different person and clearly wasn't the same woman I fell in love with and married years earlier. She was never a bad person, but she had become a different person. We no longer shared the same views on what it meant to be married.

Then came the day Angie and I met to talk about our future. She explained she had acted on her feelings and was currently dating a woman. She still loved me and wanted to be with me, but refused to give up being bisexual.

I knew then it was over between us. On some level, I could accept her liking other women, but I knew she wanted children badly. The thought of raising children in a confusing environment like that was something I wanted no part of.

This was a very difficult time for me. I truly believed in my marriage vows and couldn't believe it was turning out this way. For the first time in my life I was experiencing depression. Nothing like what my mother suffered from, but I got a glimpse of how she must feel. I understood then how a person could be made to feel so hurt, so sad and so vulnerable.

For several days I lay in bed; not wanting to move or to be around people. I couldn't bring myself to eat much. It was horrible.

The life of a professional mixed martial artist is a hard one; not only on the body, but on the pocketbook and marriage. After trying to save the situation with hours of marriage counseling, we called it quits. We didn't want the same things out of life any longer.

So my marriage ended and I was on my own again. It seemed I had gone full circle and was back where I started—in Japan and all alone.

Chapter Twenty-one

Eriko

So there I was living in Tokyo and single again. I had done so much but somehow ended up right back where I had started. More importantly, the goal posts had shifted dramatically, as I would soon discover.

I finally received permanent residence in Japan in July of 2008. Permanent residency meant that I would no longer need to teach English just to be able to stay in Japan and work legally.

Understandably, following the divorce, I slumped into a depression. I felt like the world was punishing me. I had taken my vows in marriage seriously and was deeply saddened by the fact that my bond with Angie had not been strong enough to sustain us while we worked through our difficulties. While the timing may have been questionable, I wanted to try and move on with my life so I made the decision to start dating again.

Her name was Terasawa Eriko and she was born and raised in Tokyo. We shared a bond of being the children of two educators. Her father was a professor at Tokyo University (the Japanese equivalent of Harvard) and her mother was a high school teacher. Both her parents were equally invested in teaching the younger generation; the future of Japan.

As the only daughter among three siblings, Eriko's parents had a tendency to be strict. In Japan it is common that romantic interests not be introduced to the parents until marriage had been proposed and accepted. Thus, she kept her personal life private from her family.

With a failed marriage behind me, I was adamant about building a strong friendship first. Eriko and I started to spend a lot of time together. Over the course of several months, we became closer and closer.

Before fights, it had been my norm to put my life on hold and focus solely on training. Each fight had its own intricacies and required my complete attention. I often went a month or two without seeing anyone, except my training partners.

One day, after receiving notification about an upcoming fight, I was preparing to enter the intensive pre-fight training period and therefore explained to Eriko that my time would be limited over the next month or two. When I arrived at the park the next day for my morning run, I was surprised to see her already there, ready to run beside me. I didn't think she would be able to keep up, but she surpassed my expectations and kept pace throughout the workout.

Eriko would not only eventually become my girlfriend; she also became a regular training partner. At 5 am we ran five to ten miles, followed by strength training and agility drills each day prior to my fights. We ate, slept, and trained together. Without the need to separate myself to focus on my training and a mutual joy for working out, we became inseparable.

* * * * *

Although Angie and I were now divorced, she still lived at the apartment in Koshigaya that we had both shared. In order to rent an apartment in Japan, you need a guarantor; a co-signer to assume the risk in case something should leave the person(s) living in the apartment, unable to pay rent.

A friend of mine, Kato Masato was the guarantor for our Koshigaya apartment. When Angie and I divorced, I suggested that we change the guarantor; take Kato-san's name off of the lease because I would no longer be living there.

Over the course of the next couple of months, Angie suddenly started to avoid my calls and had failed to submit the new guarantor information to the landlord. Unfortunately as a result, Kato-san found himself in a difficult situation. I think the whole thing became tiring for him and he chose to distance himself from us; from me. I understood his decision but, sincerely regretted that it had come to that. I valued his friendship.

Kato-san was a former pitcher for the Yokohama Bay Stars. Baseball is very popular in Japan. After retiring, he opened and ran a successful sports massage business in Yokohama. He and I had been talking about forming a company together and opening a MMA gym. Due to the fallout we had over the apartment in Koshigaya, the plan never materialized. It would have been a dream-come-true for me.

The Japanese government does not make it easy for foreigners to set up a company. Renting a commercial location can be extremely costly, and without a partner or sponsor, it was not possible. There was the added complication of simply finding a landlord willing to rent to a foreigner.

That's when, despite having received permanent residency, I made the important decision to return to America.

By this time I had become so accustomed to Japan that I was literally scared of returning to America to live. Visiting was one thing, but actually living and working there was something different.

The decision wasn't easy for me. In fact, I agonized over it for weeks and not for the reasons you might think. The problem was I hadn't lived in the States for such a long time that just the thought of learning to live in a culture that was nothing more than a distant memory by then, had me worried. *How am I supposed to find of job if I've dropped out of college and have no relevant work history in the U.S.?* To make matters worse, Michigan's economy had been hit hard and unemployment was at an all-time high. I would be a stranger in my own country.

On the other hand, it might just be the perfect opportunity to start a business; to relocate Kaminari Dojo to America. A bad economy also meant that commercial space could be obtained at a low price.

My mother had been struggling to get healthy. A couple years earlier she had had a knee replacement surgery. After the fact, she came to find out that a mistake had been made and she was not recovering as well as she should have. After seeking a second opinion from a specialist, it was decided that she would need to have a revision done; they would need to operate again.

Knowing how hard it was for her to recover properly after her first surgery, I knew it was time to go home; to return to Grand Rapids to be with her during her time of need.

However, I knew that caring for my mother while trying to build a business would be challenging. My close relationship with Eriko also weighed heavily on my mind.

Eriko and I sat at a café one day and I told her that I would be returning to America. I wasn't sure what would happen to us. It was then that we made the decision not to let the distance end our relationship. Although she had a job and her own obligations in Japan, Eriko offered to accompany me to Grand Rapids to help me care for my mother while I got the business off the ground.

* * * * *

In September of 2008, just four months before I returned to America, I finally had the opportunity to work for the UFC, although not in the way I had originally hoped. My good friend and long time training partner, Chonan Ryo had signed with the UFC. I accompanied him to Atlanta, GA to interpret and corner him in his fight vs. Roan Carneiro, a tough Brazilian jiu-jitsu black belt. Chonan had beaten Carneiro in a controversial fight in Deep three years earlier.

After a 14-hour flight, Chonan and I finally arrived in Atlanta just a few days before the fight. We met up with

Ryan Parsons and Jason "Mayhem" Miller. The three of us would be cornering Chonan. Chonan had befriended Dan Henderson, Ryan, and Jason after he and Dan fought in Pride. Subsequently, he had spent some time training with them in Temecula, CA at Dan's gym, Team Quest Mixed Martial Arts & Fitness.

In the days leading up to the event, Chonan had to go through a lot of media duties. Sometimes, I don't think the fans realize how much goes into getting ready to fight. The media duties seemed to never end. Luckily, Chonan took it in stride and seemed unfazed as I interpreted and did the voice over commentary as they filmed his pre-fight video shoot.

On the day of the event, we were backstage helping Chonan get warmed up. One of UFC's personnel entered the room and told Chonan he was up next.

As he made his way to the cage, Ryan, Jason and I followed. The noise of the crowd was deafening. MMA had come a long ways in America and the fans had finally embraced it!

Chonan went on to win a hard fought three-round battle with Roan Carneiro; proving once and for all that his win over Carneiro in Deep wasn't a fluke. He fought well and we were proud of him!

* * * * *

When we returned to Japan, I only had a few months to get things in order to return to America.

The day before I returned home to Grand Rapids, I met up with Chonan and some other friends for a going-away party. I'm not much of a drinker; in fact, I rarely drink at all. However, we were celebrating, and in Japan no celebration is complete without alcohol.

We met up at an *Izakaya*, a type of Japanese drinking establishment that serves food to accompany the drinks. My drink of choice was *Oolonghai*.

Oolonghai has an acquired taste. It is a mixture of the Chinese black tea called *Oolong* and *Shochu*, a strong Japanese form of alcohol that is distilled from barley, sweet potatoes, or rice.

We spent hours reminiscing. Having encountered so many difficult things in Japan, this reminded me that the good friends I'd made would miss me.

I awoke the next morning and made my way to the Narita International Airport. I would leave first and Eriko planned to come the following week. It saddened me to be leaving a country I'd called home for the better part of twelve years. However, it was time to go home. My mother needed me. I reminded myself of the fact that I had permanent residency and could easily return one day. Tears trickled down by face as the plane took off...

* * * * *

Back home in Grand Rapids, my mother had just come out of surgery when I arrived, so I rushed to be by her side. She wept tears of joy when I reached her bedside. I was finally home. We could now make up for all those years we spent away from each other.

Doctors advised my mother to stay off her feet for extended periods of time to allow her knee time to heal. I did my best to help by preparing meals, cleaning the house, and making sure she had warm blankets.

Happily, my mother would eventually make a full recovery from her surgery and be back to her old self. I was also happy to know that there were new medications to help control her mental illness so it no longer impacted her life as heavily.

* * * * *

Each day presented me with a new challenge. Readjusting to American life would take time. I had never lived in America as an adult.

Grand Rapids is a big city with a small town mentality. I

hadn't prepared myself for this and initially found it hard to find common ground in conversation. In Japan, some things are better left unsaid. In America, people are more vocal about their opinions. Whether it's sex, religion, or politics, it's common for people to voice their opinion to others even if they do not share the same beliefs. Suddenly, I felt like I was being judged on my every word. My experiences in life were not the same as those around me and many times we saw things differently.

It was happening all over again; those same feelings I initially had in Japan were back, stronger than ever.

To be honest, without Eriko by my side, I am not so sure the transition to life back in the U.S. would have been successful. Most likely I would have returned to Japan after my mother had recovered. Everything was too different… I was too different… Eriko was where I turned to be understood.

* * * * *

With the help of my childhood kung fu teacher, Sifu Sam Hing Fai Chan, I started teaching MMA at Chan's Kung Fu School again. This time it was under the business name of "Kaminari Dojo." Sifu was more than my teacher; he was now my mentor, as well. I learned more from him over our simmering hot cups of coffee in the morning than I ever could have hoped for; more than I would have learned in college to be sure. In business, you have to get your feet wet, so to speak. It is one thing to read about doing it, and quite another to actually do it.

Eight short months after starting to teach at Chan's Kung Fu School, I had enough students to support my decision to lease a space and start what would hopefully become a house-hold name for MMA in Western Michigan: Kaminari Dojo Mixed Martial Arts Academy.

Eriko and I worked hard day in and day out to get the

building in order. We laid the mats, prepared the window signage, and advertised the best we could, utilizing everything we'd learned from Sifu.

With Sifu's blessing, in October of 2009, we opened the doors to the public for the first time. We'd done it. Kaminari Dojo was now open for business!

I like to think fighting had prepared me for this situation, giving me a frame of mind that failure was not an option. Having experienced hardship constantly as a foreigner in Japan first-hand, it gave me a whole new appreciation for what America stood for and was all about. The American dream was real. It was like a breath of fresh air to finally be rewarded for all my hard work.

Chapter Twenty-two

Until Death Do Us Part

I would love to be able to say that Eriko and I are now married with two lovely children…but unfortunately; the world has not been that kind.

Eriko and I were engaged to be married in June of 2010. Due to some initial resistance from her family and difficulty for her to continue her tourism career from Grand Rapids, Eriko decided to spend a year in the French colony, New Caledonia, off the coast of Australia. She would be working at a 5-star hotel before we married.

While paddle boarding on her day off, Eriko lost her board at sea. She lost her battle against the ocean's strength and passed away on April 13th, 2012.

I visited her grave in Japan to say good-bye to the woman I loved. It took some time for me to find where she was laid to rest, but once I did, I started crying uncontrollably. The feelings I had for Eriko overwhelmed me and in a voice overcome by sadness, I wept the words *"Nande Shinundayo…?"* *"Eriko ga inai to ore wa dame dayo…"* (Why did you die…? How am I supposed to live without you…?)

I sat down to try and calm myself but couldn't stop crying. I must have startled some people because a mother and son came to see what the noise was. When they saw me crying, they left the scene to give me some space.

A Japanese gentleman, my elder by many decades, passed by me. He was there visiting a grave nearby; I assumed that of his late wife. As he passed, he nodded in my direction and said *"Konnichiwa…* (Good afternoon…) ". I responded likewise in my sad voice.

Right then and there, nationality was of no significance. We were simply two human beings mourning the death of a loved one. A calm came over me while I said my last goodbye to Eriko and whispered the words "I love you," as I touched her grave.

Chapter Twenty-three

Final Thoughts

A message to those interested in visiting or living in Japan

Japan is a wonderful country and a wonderful place to experience life.

Many of us get held up on the "what ifs" in life. What if I don't know the language? What if I can't find a job? I could go on and on.

One thing I have learned is that life has a way of working out if you work hard. Don't let these thoughts hold you back. Travel and see the country. See the world.

By all means, learn the language! In my opinion, you cannot experience "real Japan" without learning the language. It will give you insight into the people and their customs. It will also open doors that you may not have been aware of. Through the language, you will learn and truly understand why things are done the way they are.

I wish you luck on your journey.

A message to those with aspirations of competing in the sport of MMA

You have a long road ahead of you. At the time of this writing, Japan has lost its position as the mecca of MMA. I would not recommend moving to Japan to enrich your career.

Now, generally speaking, America has the best athletes and the best gyms and coaching staff in the world.

149

I suggest that you find a gym and build a relationship with the fighters and coaches by withstanding the test of time. From the beginning, join with the intention to dedicate yourself for as long as it takes to get noticed.

Don't be afraid to invest in yourself. If you are unwilling to give it your all, why should anyone else invest their time in you or believe in you?

Times have changed. There is a lot of money to be made in the sport now. For a select few, millions of dollars can be earned.

An opportunity to reach the top does not come along very often. Don't rush it. Take your time to perfect your technique. The game is constantly evolving, so evolve with it.

Fight each fight as if it were your last. It is my firm belief that if you give it your all, eventually, you will be rewarded.

Good luck and train hard!

Connect with Ryan Bow

For updates, pictures, and much more

PLEASE CONNECT WITH RYAN HERE:

The Blog of Ryan Bow:

www.ryanbow.com/

Tunnel Visions:
Memoirs of a Mixed Martial Arts Champion:

www.facebook.com/memoirsofammachampion

CPSIA information can be obtained at www.ICGtesting.com
Printed in the USA
LVOW101716020613

336550LV00014B/111/P